OUTLINE STUDIES
IN ECOLOGY

MODELLING

JOHN N. R. JEFFERS

Other titles in this series

Island Ecology	M. Gorman
Plant–Atmosphere Relationships	John Grace
Insect Herbivory	I.D. Hodkinson and M.K. Hughes
Vegetation Dynamics	John Miles
Animal Population Dynamics	R. Moss, A. Watson and J. Ollason

Outline

Editors

George M. Dunnet
Regius Professor of Natural Hist
University of Aberdeen

Charles H. Gimingham
Professor of Botany,
University of Aberdeen

Editors' Foreword

Both in its theoretical and applied aspects, ecology is developing rapidly. In part because it offers a relatively new and fresh approach to biological enquiry, but it also stems from the revolution in public attitudes towards the quality of the human environment and the conservation of nature. There are today more professional ecologists than ever before, and the number of students seeking courses in ecology remains high. In schools as well as universities the teaching of ecology is now widely accepted as an essential component of biological education, but it is only within the past quarter of a century that this has come about. In the same period, the journals devoted to publication of ecological research have expanded in number and size, and books on aspects of ecology appear in ever-increasing numbers.

These are indications of a healthy and vigorous condition, which is satisfactory not only in regard to the progress of biological science but also because of the vital importance of ecological understanding to the well-being of man. However, such rapid advances bring their problems. The subject develops so rapidly in scope, depth and relevance that textbooks, or parts of them, soon become out-of-date or inappropriate for particular courses. The very width of the front across which the ecological approach is being applied to biological and environmental questions introduces difficulties: every teacher handles his subject in a different way and no two courses are identical in content.

This diversity, though stimulating and profitable, has the effect that no single text-book is likely to satisfy fully the needs of the student attending a course in ecology. Very often extracts from a wide range of books must be consulted, and while this may do no harm it is time-consuming and expensive. The present series has been designed to offer quite a large number of relatively small booklets, each on a restricted topic of fundamental importance which is likely to constitute a self-contained component of more comprehensive courses. A selection can then be made, at reasonable cost, of texts appropriate to particular courses or the interests of the reader. Each is written by an acknowledged expert in the subject, and is intended to offer an up-to-date, concise summary which will be of value to those engaged in teaching, research or applied ecology as well as to students.

Studies in Ecology

Modelling

JOHN N.R. JEFFERS

Director
Institute of Terrestrial Ecology
Merlewood Research Station
Grange-over-Sands
Cumbria

CHAPMAN AND HALL
LONDON NEW YORK

First published 1982
by Chapman and Hall Ltd
11 New Fetter Lane, London EC4P 4EE
Published in the USA
by Chapman and Hall
733 Third Avenue, New York NY 10017

© 1982 J.N.R. Jeffers

Printed in Great Britain by
J.W. Arrowsmith Ltd, Bristol

ISBN 0 412 24360 1

British Library Cataloguing in Publication Data

Jeffers, J.N.R.
   Modelling.—(Outline studies in ecology)
   1. Biology—Mathematical models
   I. Title   II. Series
   574′.00724   QH323.5

   ISBN 0-412-24360-1

Library of Congress Cataloging in Publication Data

Jeffers, John Norman Richard.
   Modelling.
   (Studies in ecology)
   Bibliography: p.
   Includes index.
   1. Ecology—Mathematical models. I. Title.
II. Series: Studies in ecology (Chapman and Hall)
QH541.15.M3J433   1982   574.5′0724   82-9401
ISBN 0-412-24360-1 (pbk.)   AACR2

Contents

1   What is a model?

1.1 The concept of models

What do I mean by the word 'model', as it is used in this book? We all know what a model is in everyday language, although there may sometimes be some confusion between small three-dimensional representations of railways, roads, cities, vehicles, armies, etc., and those glamorous (and often partly undressed) ladies used in advertisements for clothes and other articles. Needless to say, I am not using the word in either of these two senses. Instead, I will use a somewhat extended interpretation which has been given to the word by scientists, as the representation of relationships between some formally defined quantities or qualities.

Scientists' use of the word in this way has a long history. It began with the attempt to express in physical terms the complex inter-relationships between man and his environment in the hope of understanding these relationships. Early models of the solar system, for example, tried to predict the movement of the visible planets around the Earth, but without success. Only later was it found to be possible to predict these movements approximately by physical models in which the planets, including Earth, moved round the Sun. Both of these models, however, were true physical models known as orreries, so-called after the Earl of Orrery who lived around 1700 A.D. Similar attempts were made in the early history of science to use purely physical models as analogues of observed relationships in man's experience. These early scientists believed that the understanding necessary to build such models was sufficient for the understanding of the phenomena themselves, even to the extent of building automata in the hope of understanding the ultimate mystery of man.

As man's experience and intellect grew, however, scientists were no longer content with the explanations which could be derived from physical models, and the development of mathematics enabled many of these physical models to be replaced by mathematical expressions of formal relationships. The geometry of Pythagoras was a triumph for man's intellect, enabling him to replace trial and error methods of building by exact calculation and prediction. Similarly, the development of the infinitesimal calculus by Newton opened the way for mathematical models to replace physical models of the movement of objects in time and space. The concept of a 'model' was transferred from physical representations to mathematical expressions of the relationships between defined entities.

7

It is not always appreciated just how big a step in scientific thinking was this transfer from physical to conceptual and mathematical models, and the subject of mathematics is seldom taught in a way which emphasizes the role of mathematical models in extending our experience. Most of the mathematical representation which we learn in the early stages of our education is simple and straightforward, so that the advantages of transferring experience from direct physical experimentation to indirect experiments with models are slight. Only when the models, and their underlying mathematics, become relatively complex, and the results of our experiments with the models contrary to our intuitive expectations, do we begin to appreciate the advantages to be gained by their use.

Modelling in this sense represents an approach to the solution of scientific problems which has grown rapidly during the last 30 years, both in its range of application and in its complexity. In part, this development has been stimulated by the new possibilities opened up through the use of electronic computers, and, in part, the development depends upon the new theories in mathematics and systems analysis which were themselves also stimulated by the computers. The computers have become cheaper, smaller, and increasingly more powerful in terms of their speed of computation and the amounts of information which they can hold. Perhaps even more important, the algorithmic languages on which computers depend for their instructions have become a medium for the exchange of ideas about mathematical models and their application. Simply because these algorithms have to be explicit and unambiguous if the computer is to work at all, the same algorithms are capable of transferring information from one human mind to another without ambiguity. In recent years, therefore, we have seen an unprecedented explosion of new theories which are capable of being incorporated into scientific research. The purpose of this outline is to give some indication of the nature and value of such models. We shall also hope to give some guidance to those seeking to make use of modelling in their scientific research.

1.2 Word models

Before examining some simple examples of mathematical models, it is perhaps worth asking why mathematics has had such an important role to play in the construction of models. The reason is a straightforward one, but requires some explanation for the non-mathematician. Quite simply, mathematics is a language designed to show the relationships between defined entities. It is the power of the language to abstract the essential elements that is the reason for its existence. Because mathematics is a language which replaces words and concepts by symbols, difficulties of incorrect interpretation by different individuals are minimized, even when those individuals do not speak the same verbal language. Furthermore, the symbolic notation of mathematics is capable of expressing ideas of great complexity. It is perfectly possible, for example, to represent movement in space of more than four dimensions, even though such representation cannot be expressed visually to the human mind. Similarly, it is possible to manipulate descriptions of abstract elements with many variables to show the effects of feedback (defined later!) and of non-linearity. No other language has this ability, quite simply because mathematics is the language which was invented and developed to represent such relationships.

While it is true that words can be used to represent all of the experiences that are capable of being detected by the human mind, as is evident from the vast literary heritage of all the nations of the Earth, they do not achieve this representation very efficiently. The main reason for this lack of efficiency is the difficulty of expressing relationships between the defined entities, and, indeed, much story telling and literature deliberately uses ambiguity to create moods and atmosphere. Furthermore, one human mind does not necessarily interpret the words in exactly the same way as another human mind. This difference does not matter for many kinds of literature – each person is able to derive his or her own interpretation from what has been read. Ambiguity and the lack of precise meaning, however, are barriers to the transfer of information about physical relationships, and the language of mathematics was invented to overcome these barriers. For many purposes, it is also desirable to replace the words by abstract entities to make our statements about relationships more general. Thus,

$$2 \text{ pencils} + 5 \text{ pencils} = 7 \text{ pencils}$$

is obviously true. If we replace the word 'pencils' by x, the statement is generalized to $2x + 5x = 7x$ and the x can now be used for any other entity. Most of the abstraction used in modelling is obviously more complex than this example, but the principle is the same. An excellent introduction to algebraic relationships of this type is given by McKeague [1].

It should not be concluded from this brief argument that word models are of no use to the scientist. Indeed, we shall consider the use of verbal descriptions of models as a useful preliminary to more mathematical kinds of modelling. They provide us with a start to the modelling process and with a way of ensuring that everyone concerned with the development of a model is clear about the purpose of the investigation. They help to ensure that there is general agreement about at least some of the features which the eventual model should have, or they help to distinguish the features about which there is lack of agreement between those involved in the investigation. If we are wise, we will also make the attempt to translate our final model into a verbal description at the end of our research! Not only is this necessary for the understanding of those who do not know much about mathematics – including those from whom we expect support for future research – but interpretation in this way may help us to avoid mistakes.

1.3 Definition of model

Our definition of the word *model*, as it will be used in this book, is then as a *formal expression of the relationship between defined entities in physical or mathematical terms.* This definition does not exclude the possibility of the expression of the relationship in physical terms, but most of this book will be concerned solely with mathematical expressions.

It is important to note that the definition restricts the relationship to that between defined entities. Modelling is not a branch of pure mathematics, which is concerned with the deductive logic of relationships between totally abstract entities. While modelling uses the logic of mathematics, it starts from carefully defined entities, and therefore is an application of mathematics to the real world, in our case to ecology. The word 'formal' in the definition is included to indicate that the expression must ultimately be capable of being tested against reality, as a validation of the implied relationships. The expression must be capable of making predictions against which such a test can be made. Modelling is not therefore a purely theoretical exercise, but a part of the formal logic of the scientific method.

1.4 Examples

Before looking more closely at the reasons for the use of modelling in scientific enquiry, it may be helpful to look briefly at some examples of models which have been used in the past to help in the solution of ecological problems. Perhaps one of the best-known applications of such models is in the analysis of predator–prey systems. Volterra [2] described the interactions between the numbers of a population of prey species (x) and the numbers of a population of predator species (y) by a pair of simultaneous differential equations:

$$dx/dt = ax - bx^2 - cxy$$
$$dy/dt = ey + c'xy$$

where dx/dt and dy/dt are the amounts of change in the sizes of the populations of x and y, respectively, for a very small change in time t, and a, b, c, e, and c′ are constants. This simple test of equations can be shown to behave in a very similar way to populations of a prey species with a single predator, where the density of the species (i.e. the number of individuals per unit area) can be represented adequately by a single variable, where the effects of the interactions between species are nearly instantaneous, and where, in the absence of predation, the prey species would follow a logistic growth function, with an intrinsic rate of increase and a carrying capacity defined by the ratio of the constant a/b.

A further assumption is that the rate at which the prey are eaten is proportional to the product of the densities of the predator and the prey.

Analytical solution of these equations shows that both predator and prey numbers oscillate with decreasing amplitude, the predator oscillations lagging in phase behind the prey. If b = 0, the prey species is limited only by the predator, and the prey increases exponentially in the absence of the predator. The oscillations are of constant amplitude, depending only on the initial conditions. A system converges to a steady state, with prey and predator both present, only when the carrying capacity (a/b) is high enough to support the predator. A system started close to its steady state will have small amplitude oscillations, and one started far from its steady state will have large amplitude oscillations. The behaviour of such systems is illustrated in Model 1. Beginning from a simple model of this kind, it is possible to develop models with more complex relationships between prey and predator species [3].

Another simple mathematical relationship which is frequently used in modern ecology is the multiple linear regression model, characterized by the equation:

$$y = a + b_1 x_1 + b_2 x_2 + b_3 x_3 + \ldots b_p x_p$$

where y is a random variable distributed about a mean that is dependent on the values of the p variables $x_1, x_2, \ldots, x_p$. It is assumed that these variables affect only the mean of y, and that the variance is constant. The constant a, and the coefficients $b_1, b_2, \ldots, b_p$, are usually estimated by what is known as a minimum least-squares procedure, that is by fitting a straight line through a series of given data values in such a way

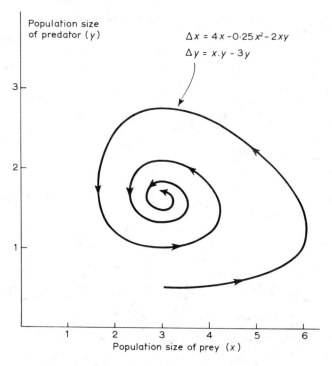

Population size of predator (y)

$\Delta x = 4x - 0.25 x^2 - 2xy$

$\Delta y = x.y - 3y$

Population size of prey (x)

Model 1 Volterra predator–prey model

that the sum of squares of deviations from the line to the given values of y is minimized. Under certain conditions, this procedure is relatively straightforward and easy to calculate [4–7].

As an example of this multiple regression model, the following equation was derived from a series of measurements of the deposition of airborne sulphur at 17 locations in Scotland and northern England:

$$S' = -62.9 + 0.159E + 0.121N - 0.000\,147E^2 - 0.000\,073N^2 - 0.000\,079E.N + 0.003\,06R$$

where S' is the 'excess' wet deposition in sulphur in kg/ha/yr, E is the Easting of the National Grid km, N is the Northing of the National Grid km, and R is the precipitation in mm.

The model accounts for 77% of the observed variability in the total wet deposition of sulphur, with a standard deviation from regression of 1.46 kg/ha/yr. Model 2 shows how wet deposition of sulphur varies with geographical location.

Model 2 Regression model of 'excess' wet deposition of sulphur in Scotland and N. England

Site	Grid co-ordinates		Precipita-tion (mm)	'Excess' wet deposition of $S(kg/ha/yr)$	
	E	N		Observed	Predicted
Achnagoichan	291	808	785	3.6	4.86
Banchory	369	795	892	6.0	5.37
Betty Hill	270	961	801	0.7	0.13
Bush	324	663	792	6.6	6.77
Broadford	164	823	1085	1.5	2.02
Devilla	295	688	733	7.1	6.12
Faskally	292	760	909	3.9	6.04
Forest of Deer	397	850	1368	3.2	4.69
Inverpolly	209	912	1187	1.1	2.12
Lephinmore	200	692	1831	5.5	6.46
Lochnagar	325	785	965	4.0	6.05
Nigg Bay	396	804	596	3.3	3.78
Redesdale	383	695	794	7.3	6.67
Rowardennan	235	698	1778	9.9	7.72
Springburn	260	668	1066	5.4	6.30
Torlundy	215	777	1435	4.3	5.63
Windermere	341	498	1127	5.4	6.41

Regression equation:

$$S^1 = -62.9 + 0.159E + 0.121N - 0.000\,147E^2 - 0.000\,073N^2 - 0.000\,079E.N + 0.003\,06R$$

where S' = excess wet deposition of sulphur in kg/ha/yr;
    E = Easting of National Grid;
    N = Northing of national Grid;
    R = precipitation in mm.

Equation accounts for 77% of the variability in deposition, with a standard deviation from regression of 1.46 kg/ha/yr.

Model 3 Markov model of successional changes in a raised mire

Starting state	Transitional probability (time step = 20 years)			
	Bog	Calluna	Woodland	Grazed
Bog	0.65	0.29	0.06	0.00
Calluna	0.30	0.33	0.30	0.07
Woodland	0.00	0.28	0.69	0.03
Grazed	0.00	0.40	0.20	0.40

Calculated equilibrium proportions

Bog	Calluna	Woodland	Grazed
0.22	0.25	0.38	0.15

Mean first passage times (years)

From	To			
	Bog	Calluna	Woodland	Grazed
Bog	—	71	144	634
Calluna	191	—	105	575
Woodland	273	82	—	584
Grazed	373	182	100	—

Finally, Model 3 gives the transition probabilities for a simple Markov model of the successional changes in a raised mire. A first-order Markov model is one in which the future development is determined by the present state of the system and is assumed to be independent of the way in which that state has developed. The transition probabilities therefore show the probabilities that any area of raised mire, which is in one of the four starting states of bog, *Calluna* heath, woodland, or grazed, will have moved to one of the other states during one time step of 20 years. Appropriate analysis of models of this kind can reveal any state of equilibrium that will eventually be reached by the habitats. It will also determine the average length of time taken for an area of bog to become *Calluna*-dominated, woodland or grazed, or, if we choose an area at random, the average lengths of time we would need to wait for this area to become bog, *Calluna*, woodland or grazed.

It must be emphasized that these examples have been described briefly and out of the context of their practical application in order to clarify the sense in which we use the word 'model' in this book. We must now turn our attention to reasons for making and using models of this kind, and to the important stages in the development of models for particular purposes.

2 Why do I need a model?

2.1 Reason for use of models

Some of the reasons for using models in scientific research have already been mentioned in the last chapter. The need for simple ways of expressing the relationships between basic entities in the search for a solution to a problem encourages us to use a language capable of making abstractions from the complexity of the world we are trying to understand. Many of these problems are too complex to be solved by commonsense rules of thumb or by intuition, and the use of words by themselves is not usually a satisfactory way of describing relationships. We use models because they reduce ambiguity and because they describe complexity with the maximum parsimony.

Ecological research has a particular need for the use of models because of its concern with the many-sided interactions of a wide variety of organisms. Nearly all of these interactions are dynamic, in the sense that they vary with time and are constantly changing. Furthermore, these interactions frequently possess the characteristics of 'feedback', i.e. the carrying back of some of the effects of a process to their source or to a preceding stage so as to strengthen or modify them . This feedback may be positive, in the sense that the effect is increased, or negative in the sense that the effect is decreased. Feedback may itself be complex, involving a series of positive and negative effects, with various results depending on other environmental factors.

The complexity of ecological relationships is not, however, confined to the presence of multiple interactions in the relationships between organisms. Living organisms are themselves variable – indeed, variability is one of their essential attributes. This variability may be expressed in terms of effects on other organisms, for example by competition or by predation, or it may be expressed in the response of the organisms, either collectively or singly, to environmental conditions. Such response will be reflected in variable rates of growth, and reproduction, or even in variable ability to exist under markedly adverse conditions. When this characteristic is added to independent variations in environmental factors such as climate and habitat, ecological processes become difficult to investigate and control.

As a result, the understanding of even relatively unmodified ecological systems is far from easy. The traditional response of the ecologists to the difficulty has been to focus attention on small subsets of a larger problem. Much research has been concentrated on the behaviour of single organisms in simplified habitats, for example on beetles in bags of flour, or enchytraeid worms on selected media. Alternatively, the competition between two or three species, again in relatively simple habitats, has been studied extensively. In all of these examples, an attempt is made to reduce the level of the complexity studied to a level which is manageable by traditional methods of investigation, by eliminating many of the possible sources of variability. Even when this has been done, however, the inter-relationships remain difficult to understand.

When the effects of deliberate modification of ecological systems are included in the ecological research, a further dimension of variability and interaction is introduced. Both forestry and agriculture are examples of applied ecology, in which some simplification of the ecological system is usually achieved by considering the response of the crop species alone, but such research provides very little information on the response of the system as a whole to modifications introduced by changes in management. In particular, the effects of the crop species on the soil, and on species or organisms associated with the ecosystem on which the crop has been imposed, are seldom studied, mainly because of the difficulty of designing experiments which are capable of testing hypotheses with the necessary degree of complexity. The extension of these ideas to the ecological effects of land use, where several alternative strategies for land use and environmental management are considered, is even more difficult.

For all the above reasons, i.e. the inherent complexity of ecological relationships, the characteristic variability of living organisms, and the apparently unpredictable effects of deliberate modification of ecological systems by man, the ecologist requires an orderly and logical representation of the underlying relationships. There is, however, a further reason for the use of models in ecological research. By its very nature, such research frequently requires long time-scales, measured in years rather than in weeks. It is, therefore, necessary to ensure the greatest possible advance from each stage of experimentation, and models of systems in ecology provide a useful framework for the integration and testing of the compatibility of information which is collected about the system under investigation. Especially where much of the research is undertaken by different groups of people, and in different locations, this integration and testing for compatibility becomes an important task for which the model acts as a means of communication between different research workers. This particular use of models will be discussed further later in this chapter.

A rather similar context of the use of models lies in the use of simulation as a synthesis of available information. Again, this application of models in ecological research will be discussed later in the chapter.

2.2 Complexity
As one of the reasons for using models to describe ecological relation-

16

ships has been given as complexity, it may be as well to spend a little time considering the nature of complexity in ecology, with some simple models as examples. Four principal types of complexity will be described separately, namely non-linearity, interaction, feedback and discontinuity. In many practical situations, two or more of these features may be combined.

Non-linearity is the simplest of the features to describe. A linear relationship implies a constant or proportional relationship between two or more variables. Thus, the equations:

$$y = bx$$

or

$$y = a + bx$$

both indicate a linear relationship between y and x, the value of y being changed in proportion to any change in the value of x. In contrast, the exponential growth function:

$$x_t = x_0 e^{rt} \quad \text{or} \quad x_0 \exp(rt)$$

where x is the population density at time t, x_0 is the population density when $t = 0$, and r is a constant, defines a non-linear relationship between population density (x) and time (t) as in Model 4. This growth function is often used as a simple model for the growth of a population where there are no limitations on the size of the population, e.g. for the growth of a bacterial colony before the culture medium is exhausted. Exponential growth can only continue for a limited time in most ecological situations: ultimately, an increasing population will exhaust its resources. The population may then settle down to some steady value, it may fluctuate regularly or irregularly, or it may decline. If it settles to a steady state, the logistic growth function:

$$x_t = x_0 / (1 - ke^{-rt})$$

is often used as an appropriate model, where k is the carrying capacity (Model 4).

Non-linear models of this kind are not, of course, confined to studies of the growth of populations. For example, Leith [8] has modelled the relationships between primary productivity, measured in terms of annual dry matter production, and climate by two non-linear relationships:

$$Y = 3000/(1 + \exp(1.315 - 0.119\,T))$$

and

$$Y = 3000(1 - \exp(-0.000\,64R))$$

where Y is the annual dry matter production in g/m^2, T is the mean annual temperature in °C, and R is the mean annual precipitation in mm.

17

Time	Exponential	Logistic
0	1.00	1.00
0.5	1.05	1.04
1	1.11	1.08
2	1.22	1.16
3	1.35	1.24
4	1.49	1.33
5	1.65	1.42
6	1.82	1.51
7	2.01	1.61
8	2.23	1.70
9	2.45	1.80
10	2.72	1.90
11	3.00	2.00
12	3.32	2.10
13	3.67	2.20
14	4.06	2.30

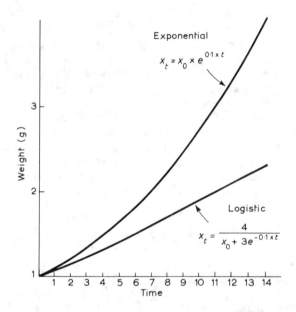

Exponential

$$x_t = x_0 \times e^{0.1 \times t}$$

Logistic

$$x_t = \frac{4}{x_0 + 3e^{-0.1 \times t}}$$

Model 4 Exponential and logistic models of the growth of a population of organisms

Using these two equations, and accepting the lowest value when the two equations give different estimates, he has been able to plot some interesting maps of the world showing potential production of dry matter, as a first approximation to a world-scale model of primary productivity. Model 5 gives estimates of annual dry matter production for some locations in Britain.

18

Location	Mean annual precipitation (mm)	Mean annual temp. (°C)	Annual dry matter production (g/m²)
Aberdeen	847	7.7	1204
Achnashellach	2161	7.9	1222
Ambleside	1902	8.9	1309
Birmingham	774	9.5	1206
Bognor Regis	738	10.3	1162
Cambridge	556	9.8	926
Cardiff	1085	10.1	1415
Dover	778	10.4	1210
Durham	650	8.5	1052
London	638	10.7	1036
Manchester	819	9.4	1258
Penzance	1098	11.3	1522
Plymouth	990	10.7	1445
Stornaway	1094	8.3	1257
Wick	788	7.7	1205

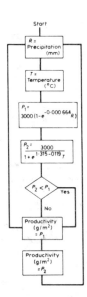

Model 5 Prediction of annual dry matter production from mean annual precipitation and temperature

Interaction, or the extent to which the effect of one factor varies with the changes in strength of other factors, is another type of complexity which frequently demands the use of models to reveal and unravel. Indeed, many of the difficulties of practical experimentation in ecological research spring from the existence of interactions, making inefficient or even completely useless simple experimental designs in which only one factor or treatment is changed at a time. The existence of interaction can often be revealed by quite simple models, such as the two-way median models described by McNeil [9] or by the analysis of variance models of more conventional statistical analysis. Model 6 gives an example of simple linear interaction between two factors, but the effects of interaction may be considerably more complex than in this simple example, and may include non-linear effects.

Feedback, or the carrying back of some of the effects of a process to their source, or to a preceding stage, so as to strengthen or modify those effects, is perhaps one of the most troublesome complications in the understanding of ecological processes. Indeed, as May [10] has shown, the existence of several feedback loops connecting even a relatively small number of variables by non-linear functions is sufficient to make the behaviour of an ecological system difficult to predict, and may make the behaviour of the system counter-intuitive. Modelling of ecological systems, therefore, tends to be concentrated on the problems of the existence or non-existence of feedback loops in the processes, especially when competition or some other limit is imposed on the growth of

19

Model 6 Two-way median model of changes in moisture content of shoots and roots of desert species

Species	July 1974		November 1974	
	Shoot	Root	Shoot	Root
Elymus farctus	36.6	13.9	31.4	32.6
Ammophila arenaria	23.3	17.3	34.9	36.2
Crucianella maritima	32.1	41.2	26.7	48.4
Pancratium arabicum	76.7	75.7	80.5	74.6
Echinops spinosissimus	53.0	43.3	44.9	52.9
Euphorbia paralias	77.8	57.1	59.7	58.2
Ononis vaginalis	24.2	40.6	21.1	39.5

$$M_{ij} = 37.4 + S_i + C_j + r_{ij}$$

	Residuals (r_{ij})				
	July		November		Species effects
Species	Shoot	Root	Shoot	Root	(S_i)
Ammophila arenaria	−2.8	−7.2	7.8	2.8	−10.5
Elymus farctus	8.3	−12.7	2.2	−2.9	−8.4
Ononis vaginalis	−4.0	14.0	−8.1	4.0	−8.4
Crucianella maritima	−4.5	6.2	−10.9	4.5	0.0
Echinops spinosissimus	7.3	−0.7	−1.7	0.0	9.0
Euphorbia paralias	19.0	0.0	0.0	−7.8	22.1
Pancratium arabicum	0.0	0.7	2.9	0.0	40.1
Column effects (C_j)	−0.8	−2.5	0.1	6.4	37.4

populations or organisms.

Discontinuity, the fourth of the types of complexity to be considered in this brief review, refers to any large change in behaviour or state associated with a relatively small change in some other variable, including time. In ecological systems, discontinuity is often associated with three other forms of complexity, namely bimodality, hysteresis, and divergence. *Bimodality* refers to the system being characterized by one or two (or more) distinct states, while the property of discontinuity implies that only relatively few (if any) individuals or observations fall between these states. The characteristic division of organisms into males and females is a good example of both bimodality and discontinuity. The presence of occasional individuals whose sex is indeterminate does not greatly hinder the recognition of the two states, but, in practical terms, there is sufficient discontinuity between the two states to enable most individuals to be placed in one of the two categories.

Hysteresis occurs when a system has an apparently delayed response to a changing stimulus, and, characteristically, the response to the stimulus follows one path when the stimulus increases and another path when the stimulus decreases. *Divergence* is more difficult to describe, but is closely related to hysteresis, in that it is characterized by nearby starting conditions evolving to widely separated final states. In applications to population dynamics, for example, initial conditions just above and just below quite well defined thresholds frequently diverge to very different final populations.

In recent years, the models of catastrophe theory have been widely used to illustrate the properties of discontinuity, divergence, bimodality, and hysteresis. Model 17 gives a simple example of a three-dimensional catastrophe theory model of an ecological problem. Most real problems are, of course, very much more complex than this example, but the direct and visual appeal of the catastrophe theory representation is evident.

2.3 Integration and testing of compatibility of information already collected about a system

What has already been said about the need for models in this chapter has assumed that you are beginning to work on a new problem in ecology, and has stressed some of the basic difficulties in ecological research, and particularly the complexity of ecological systems. In reality, it is very seldom that any research worker begins work in the absence of any existing information about the ecological system with which he or she is concerned. There will usually be a great deal of existing information contained in published papers, in unpublished reports, and in data which have been collected and stored in research files and in computer data banks. A valuable use of models in this situation is in the integration and testing of the available information and data. The kinds of questions that can then be answered by the use of models are related to the consistency of the data and theories of separate research workers, and the redundancy of data when these are extensive, as is often the case in ecological research.

The process of building models to test the compatibility of existing data and information does not differ markedly from that of building a model for an entirely new problem. Starting from one or more of the sources of information, it should be possible to construct models which incorporate the basic relationships and to fit these models to the available data. The point at which the process departs from the more direct approach to modelling is that at which it becomes necessary to test whether the various models differ from each other in any essential way. Frequently, such tests depend on statistical procedures for comparing the output from models, or for testing the hypothesis that a single model could account for the range of observed results. Model 7 shows an example of the comparison of two sets of information about the growth of yeasts in competition with each other, together with a model which combines the features of both the original models [11].

Some of the most frequent types of models for exploring existing data are those of multivariate statistical analysis which are frequently used to

21

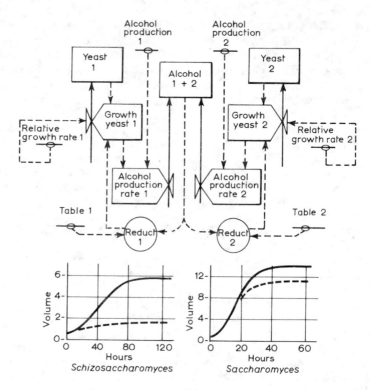

Model 7 Growth and interference of two yeast species

determine the number of independent dimensions of variability which underlie some complex field of variation. Such models are of value, for example in taxonomy, and may help to reveal where data are redundant, and where individual organisms or populations do not differ in any essential degree. Some of the large family of multivariate models are described briefly in Chapter 4, but Model 14 shows a multivariate model for the variation in leaf measurements in poplar trees as a basis for taxonomy of poplar in Britain.

Studies of variation are especially important in ecology, mainly because of the inherent property of variability in all living material, and the models of analytical statistics are therefore particularly valuable in unscrambling the sources of variability. One of the special uses of such models is in the planning of efficient schemes, designed to concentrate the largest numbers of samples where the variability is greatest and so improve the precision of the estimates made of the parameters of the sampled populations. The model of the analysis of variance and covariance which is described in most good statistical texts is therefore of special importance as a basis for further research. Model 11 gives an example of the modelling of variability at three different levels in an ecological population so as to determine the most effective structure for a sampling investigation, and identifying the variation between plots, quadrats, and between sub-samples.

2.4 Simulation as a synthesis of available information

Whether or not the models which are constructed for ecological research have been derived from an *a priori* consideration of the essential relationships between the elements of populations or processes or from the integration and testing of the compatibility of information derived from a large number of different sources, the resulting model or models may be regarded as a synthesis of the available information. Such a synthesis may then be used for further experimentation. Frequently, it is possible to test specific hypotheses about the behaviour of the system from direct tests on the model. For example, a model of the growth of a population of yeasts or bacteria may be used to test the likely effects of changes in temperature at different stages in the growth of the organisms. Jeffers *et al.* [12] give an example of a regression model used to distinguish between two alternative hypotheses about the factors determining respiration rates in soils.

Experiments on models must not be regarded as a substitute for experiments on the actual ecological system. Nevertheless, they can often be used to identify the really critical experiments which should be done to advance knowledge further, and can hence aid in making the most economical use of research resources and material. In this way, models can help in the planning of further research. When sufficient research has been done to test the models – and we will be looking at the steps that will be necessary to verify and validate models later in this book – the tested models may also be used for practical decision-making. Perhaps the most common ways in which such models are used is in the testing of possible outcomes of decisions, as in environmental impact assessment. Models may also be used, however, to find decisions which are 'optimum' in some sense, or to determine the best combination of strategies to use in a complex interaction with one or many other decision-makers, in a manner which is akin to the playing of a game. The use of such models will be explained further in Chapter 4.

3 How do I start?

3.1 Defining the problem

Modelling starts in the same way as any other scientific investigation should start – by a careful definition and bounding of the problem to be solved. It is necessary to emphasize this point because the brief history of modelling in ecology, and elsewhere, has been bedevilled by the alternative approach of looking for applications of existing models. Correctly used, however, models should be developed for problems which have been defined before any consideration is given to the type of model which will be used as a basis for the investigation. Only by being very sure about the purpose of the research, and by stating clearly and explicitly its objectives and the reasons for doing the research in the first place, can we ensure that the limited resources which we have to deploy will be correctly allocated and not dispersed into activities which are irrelevant to the problem we are meant to be addressing, and to the original universe of discourse. It also helps if the original objectives are translated into some precise questions that the research may be expected to answer.

However, it is necessary to stress here that the original definition of the problem is unlikely to be correct at the first attempt, and that there is therefore little point in aiming at perfection in one step. Once the modelling itself has begun, or even long afterwards, it may be recognized that the originally stated objectives, or, more usually, the bounds which have been set to the problem, need to be modified, so that there is a return to this stage of defining the problem. Part of the difficulty is the necessity to simplify the problem to the point at which it is likely to be capable of analytical solution, while, on the other hand, preserving all the elements which make the problem of sufficient interest for practical research. The difficult judgement of the relative importance of the inclusion or exclusion of the elements of the problem, and the balancing of their relevance to the analytical grasp of the situation against their contribution to complications which may well become unmanageable, will pose questions which will not readily be answered at the first attempt. There is a delicate balance between simplification and complexity, and retaining sufficient relationship to the original problem for the analytical solution to be recognizably appropriate will not easily be achieved. Many promising research projects have ultimately proved worthless because the complexity of the problem was allowed to swamp the subsequent modelling, with the result that it became impossible to derive a solution. In contrast, there is little point in invoking the techniques of modelling to find trivial solutions to a problem which is itself only a subset of the original problem.

In addition to the definition of the problem, it is also necessary to define the extent of the problem in both time and space. The bounding of the problem will frequently cause difficulty, mainly because most research workers are anxious to make their research as general as possible, in the sense that it applies to the widest possible range of situations and over the longest periods of time. Again, there has to be some compromise between what it is reasonable to do in a limited programme of research, and what is desirable in terms of the population about which inferences are to be made. It is, nevertheless, essential to make some decision about the extent of the intended research at this stage in the development of any kind of model.

Once the extent of the problem has been defined and bounded, it should become possible to define the goals and objectives of the investigation. Usually, these goals and objectives will form a hierarchy, with the major objectives progressively subdivided to a series of minor objectives. In such a hierarchy, it will also be necessary to determine priorities for the various stages and to determine priorities relative to the amount of effort that will be required to meet the objectives. Thus, in a complex investigation, the modeller may decide to place relatively little priority on goals and objectives which, while desirable from the point of view of scientific information, have little effect upon the decisions which may need to be made about the management of the ecological system. Alternatively, where the investigation forms part of a programme of fundamental research, he may be prepared to accept certain defined alternative forms of management and concentrate most of the efforts on objectives relative to the ecological processes themselves. For a successful model, however, it is important that the priorities that are to be assigned to various objectives should be defined clearly.

3.2 Word models

Having defined the problem as carefully as we can, and also defined the practical goals and objectives for our solution to the problem, together with the boundaries of time and space within which that solution will lie, the next stage is to attempt the most precise verbal description that we can of the problem with which we are .concerned. This kind of description, or word model, is particularly valuable when several people are collaborating on a research project. It is surprising how often even four or five people closely concerned with a problem will disagree with each other's description of the same ecological system, and disagreement on the particular elements of the system which contribute, directly or indirectly, to the problem is even more likely. There is, therefore, all the more reason to spend some time in an attempt to find an agreed description, even if that description contains some passages, expressed as alternatives, for which no agreement can be reached. Such a description may well require a return to the phases of definition and bounding of the extent of the problem, and to a re-identification of the hierarchy of goals and objectives.

The word model will need to distinguish between a population and a sample drawn from that population. In statistical terminology, the total set of individuals about which inferences are to be made is defined as a *population*. These individuals may be organisms, ecosystems, quadrats, or indeed any measure or characteristic of organisms or ecosystems. A *sample* is any finite set of individuals drawn from that population, and we will frequently assume that the sample is taken in such a way that values computed from the samples are representative of the complete population and may be regarded, therefore, as estimates of the values of the population. Characteristic values of populations are defined as *parameters*, in contrast to the corresponding values of samples which are regarded as estimates of those parameters, either as *constants* or *coefficients* in model equations. A verbal description of the problem should make the distinction between parameters and sample statistics.

A word model must also be careful to distinguish between different kinds of variables. Our model equations will contain at least two kinds of variables. One, at least, of the variables will be *dependent*, in the sense that it is a variable which is expected to be altered by changes in other variables. The other variables may be regarded as *independent* variables in the language of the differential calculus, in the sense that it is the alteration of these variables which leads to the change in the dependent variable. This use of the word 'independent' is, however, misleading as two or more independent variables may indeed be strongly correlated. A more useful distinction is to use the term '*regressor*' variables to describe those variables which provide the changes necessary to induce changes in the dependent variable.

An alternative terminology makes a distinction between *state variables*, *driving variables* and *output variables* as follows:

1. The *state variables* are defined as the measurable properties of the system, and include such values as biomass, numbers of organisms, concentration of mineral or nutrient elements, water content, and so on. The seasonal dynamics of the state variables reflect the changes taking place in the system and the values of these variables at any particular time themselves depend on changes within the system.
2. The *driving variables* are not affected by those processes internal to the system, but act upon the system from outside. In the management of natural or semi-natural systems, the most important driving variables are usually the major climatological or meteorological factors influencing the system, but biotic variables may also be considered as driving variables, for example the number of animals grazing on vegetation.
3. The *output variables* are the quantities the model is required to predict. Sometimes, these variables are a subset of the state variables, but, in addition, they will often include quantities calculated from the

27

state variables themselves. Clearly, the output variables are the quantities of most direct interest to a manager who proposes to use a model.

The models which we construct in this way will include ecological, physiological and physical processes. These processes result in changes in the state variables, and the rates at which processes take place are determined by the current or previous values of these and other state variables and of the driving variables. By describing the mechanisms of the system in this way, we can begin to see how our mathematical representation may be developed, so that the word model provides us with an introduction to the ultimate mathematical expressions which we will use in our modelling of the system.

Finally, our word model will need to connect together the various kinds of variables by some postulated relationships. It is at this point that the limitations of word models will quickly become apparent. As has been mentioned in the last chapter, it is relatively unlikely that we will be able to describe any useful ecological model purely in terms of simple linear relationships. Our word model, therefore, needs to be reasonably explicit in suggesting, at least qualitatively, the existence of non-linear relationships or interactions between two or more variables, of feedback, and of the possibility of discontinuities. If at all possible, the verbal descriptions should try to show the nature of these relationships and the direction of the effects in interactions or of feedback. It is at this point that the need for a mathematical model will be felt most acutely, and, if so, the word model has prepared us to enter into the next stage of modelling, described in the next chapter. Where possible, the verbal description that has been attempted should give an indication of possible qualitative solutions which might subsequently be compared with the quantitative solutions which we hope to derive from our more mathematical models.

One further advantage may perhaps be mentioned for the development of word models as a preliminary to the modelling and simulation of ecological systems. This is in the identification of distinct subsystems in the problem which might be examined separately and subsequently connected to form part of the larger problem. While we cannot always expect to find that every problem breaks down neatly into a series of subsystems which can be worked on relatively independently, the existence of such solutions should always be sought so as to ensure that the minimum of complexity is involved in any part of the system. Recognition of subsystems is, therefore, an important part in the preliminary examination of the problem and in its definition. Any possible subsystems should be identified in the word model, together with the ways in which the subsystem is connected to the larger system.

3.3 Diagrams
Even for the simplest applications of modelling, it may be helpful to

provide diagrams to organize, describe and simplify the relationships that are being modelled, or as a bridge between the word model and the mathematical model itself. Diagrammatic representations of relationships frequently help in the translation from words to mathematics, and provide a signpost to the mathematical analyses. For these diagrams, various conventions have been established to facilitate the description of the system and communication between other research workers.

The simplest of the conventions is that of the flow charts which have been developed by computer programmers to provide documentation allowing others to understand how and what computer programs accomplish, and to permit the logic of a complex program to be checked before the program itself is written. These flow charts use a limited number of symbols shown in Model 8. These symbols are linked together so as to show the general flow and logic of the calculations that need to be made and to demonstrate the relationships between the different variables involved in the modelling of a problem. Model 5 shows the application of simple flow charting procedures to the prediction of the annual dry matter production of vegetation.

An alternative set of conventions is given by Forrester [13], and these symbols are summarized in Model 9. They were first developed for the presentation of industrial systems, but are equally applicable to the description of ecological systems. The state variables themselves are shown by rectangles, rates of change are shown by symbols representing valves, and exogenous or driving variables by circles. Parameters or constants are shown by continuous circles on a line. The flow of material is shown by continuous arrows and the flow of information by dotted arrows. It is worth noting that these symbols do not themselves define the relationships explicitly. Such a definition is more easily achieved by the use of mathematical equations or by

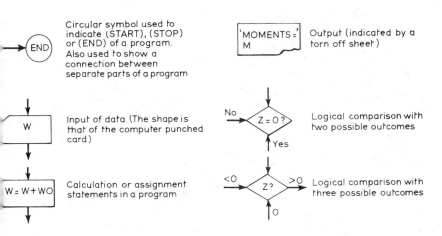

Model 8 Flow chart symbols

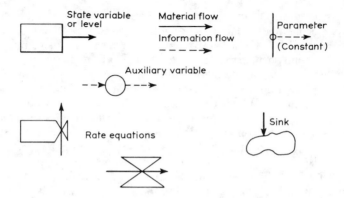

Model 9 Forrester's symbols for presentation of system inter-relationships

computer algorithms. However, many scientists find it helpful to show the main relationships symbolically as a check on the assumptions built into the mathematical expression, and frequently show a little graph of the assumed relationship beside each of the rates of change symbols.

An alternative set of conventions has been developed by Odum [14] as a series of symbols representing systems processes and mathematical functions, with their associated pathways for the transfer of energy, materials or information. These symbols are given in Model 10. In essence, they are expansions of simple box and arrow diagrams, and are intended to simplify the translation of conceptual models into computer

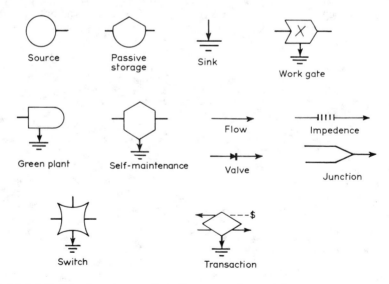

Model 10 Odum's representation of energy and material processes

languages. Using Odum's symbols, a forcing function, as a source of energy or materials from outside the system, is represented by a circle. The output from such a source may be constant, varying or intermittent. The sink symbols represent energy that must be degraded into heat during biological processes, for example through respiration and the maintenance of the metabolism of organisms. Three types of state variable are distinguished by Odum. State variables which represent massive storage, in which no new potential energy is generated in loading or unloading the variable (e.g. biomass, detritus, and photosynthetically-produced sugars), are represented by a storage tank. Self-maintaining components of a system, such as animals and decomposers, are represented as hexagons, while producers like green plants are represented by bullet-shaped symbols. As both of these last two state variables involve loss of energy, sinks must be included. Locations where one flow interacts with another are represented by work gates which indicate energy and/or material intersection points. The work gate symbol is important because it is used to show feedback loops by which systems are regulated. These intersections have many mathematical relations and these are often shown in the body of the symbol. Flow control symbols include lines, backforce, junctions, control switches, valves and monitoring transaction. It will be evident from this brief description that representation of models in Odum's notation is relatively complicated, but has the advantage that the representation carries more information than that used by Forrester [13].

4 What help can I expect from mathematics?

4.1 Mathematical notations

We have already noted the importance of the use of mathematical symbols as abstract representations of the relationships between identified entities. This use of symbols ensures freedom from subjective connotations of actual words, and also provides the ability to present very complex relationships both clearly and economically.

Most non-mathematicians have an unreasonable fear of mathematical symbols and notation. One of the first tasks of the would-be modeller, therefore, is to lose that fear, and to gain some facility in the use of symbols. Essentially, this use of symbols is like learning a language and has similar characteristics. The use of symbols, like a language, cannot be learnt all at once. It is essential to start with a few simple concepts and phrases, and then to improve one's knowledge of the language with use and practice. Thereafter, facility in the use of symbols can be developed gradually in both scope and understanding. It is not possible to teach the use of mathematical notation in this outline, and references will be given to helpful books. However, half an hour with a good teacher can often help more than many hours of reading papers and text-books.

Perhaps the most important fact to stress here is that there is more than one notation in mathematics, just as there may be more than one dialect of a language in a country. These notations are often consistent with each other in a certain sense, but they are usually directed towards different purposes and end results. Again, it is not necessary to learn all of these dialects at once. As with human languages, the second is easier to learn than the first, the third easier to learn than the second, etc., until it becomes relatively easy to learn any new notation that is required. Also, the beginner needs to be aware that notations are not always completely standardized, although the modeller should, wherever possible, adopt the conventions that are accepted by most scientists. It is dangerous to depart from these conventions unless you are very sure of what you are doing, or unless you have no interest in communicating the results of your own research to other people.

4.1.1 Arithmetic, algebraic equations and equalities

Any study of mathematical notation must necessarily begin with the symbols and notation of ordinary arithmetic, and then progress to the notation of elementary algebra where values are substituted by letters or symbols, and incorporated in equations or expressions of inequality. An *expression* is a sequence of numbers, letters, and mathematical signs which yields a certain numerical value if the letters are replaced by numbers which can be freely chosen within the domain of definition. Thus:

$$L\,(x,\,y) = \mathrm{a}x + \mathrm{b}y + \mathrm{c}$$

is a linear expression in the variables x and y, if a, b, and c can be regarded as constants. If the mathematical expressions are connected by one of the ordering symbols:

$$<, \; \leqslant, \; >, \; \geqslant$$

(standing for less than, less than or equal to, greater than, greater than or equal to, respectively), the resulting position is referred to as an *inequality*. For example:

$$2x > y.$$

The complexity of mathematical expressions is increased by the use of indices and of subscripts, but the rules for their construction and manipulation, as well as for the solution of sets of equations, are easily learnt with the aid of one of the many excellent elementary text-books. McKeague [1] can be particularly recommended to anyone needing to start from the beginning.

4.1.2 *Differential and integral calculus*

Once a reasonable facility has been gained with the manipulation and solution of algebraic expressions, including the expansion of powered functions, the extraction of factors, the summing of arithmetic, geometric and harmonic progressions, and the determination of numbers of permutations and combinations, some facility with the notation of the differential and integral calculus is highly desirable. Grossman [15] and Flanders *et al.* [16] provide useful and comprehensive introductions.

The differential calculus is concerned with the behaviour of arithmetic expressions in response to very small changes in one or more variables. The integral calculus, in contrast, is concerned with the summing of large numbers of small changes to determine the behaviour of the resulting function. In general, integration is more difficult than differentiation and involves a wider variety of mathematical manipulations. In both differential and integral calculus, special symbols are used and these must be properly understood if the modeller is to gain any facility in the arguments expressed by their use.

Equations involving several variables, and functions of these variables and their derivatives are called differential equations. Ordinary differential equations are conditional equations for a function of an independent variable which contain at least one derivative of the unknown function with respect to the independent variable. Partial differential equations are conditional equations for a function of several independent variables which contain at least one derivative of the unknown function with respect to one of the independent variables. The solution (integral) of a differential equation is defined as the set of all functions whose derivatives identically satisfy the differential equation. The general solution of a differential equation of nth order is a set of all functions, the solution of which contains exactly n arbitrary parameters or constants. A particular solution of a differential equation is obtained if, by imposition of additional initial or boundary conditions, the values of these parameters are specified. A solution of a differential equation is called singular if it cannot be obtained from the general solution by the choice of a special parameter. Facility in the setting up of differential equations and in finding their solutions is important for anyone contemplating the use of mathematical models, but has been greatly simplified by the advent of the electronic computer, using methods which will be described briefly in the following chapter.

4.1.3 Matrix algebra

A matrix is a rectangular arrangement of numbers enclosed in parentheses. A capital, bold-faced letter is used in formulae to represent a matrix, and the corresponding lower case letter with appropriate subscripts is used to represent any element of that matrix.

The advantages of expressing arrays of numbers as matrices is that these arrays can be manipulated in ways which are analogous to the manipulation of ordinary numbers, or scalars. For example, the addition or subtraction of two matrices corresponds to the addition or subtraction of each corresponding element of the matrix. Multiplication and division of matrices are more complex, but remain unambiguous mathematical operations. The notation of matrix algebra is, therefore, one of the most important developments of modern mathematics, and the modeller is recommended to study one or more of the available introductory text-books, for example Searle [17], Anton [18], Rorres and Anton [19], and Strong [20].

4.1.4 Set theory and Boolean algebra

When we collect all objects possessing a certain property into an aggregate, the aggregation is called a *set*, provided it can be uniquely determined whether or not any one of these objects has the specified property. The set of the natural numbers:

$$N = (0; 1; 2; \ldots)$$

and the set of the whole numbers:

$$I = (0; 1; -1; 2; -2; \ldots).$$

If the elements of sets are points of a curve, a plane, or a space, the sets are also called *point sets*. If each element a_i of set A is contained in set B, then set A is a subset of B. Mathematicians have developed a special notation to indicate the union, intersection, and Cartesian product of sets, and this special notation is often useful in some aspects of modelling.

Similarly, the Boolean algebra was created as a calculus for the description of logical relations that mathematically symbolize the statements as true or false. Its development into a two-value Boolean algebra, or switching algebra, is based on the fact that computers use techniques with storage-free binary elements which only have two possible states, either 'on' or 'off'. As a result, the special Boolean algebra has become particularly useful in modelling through the use of electronic computers. Some introductory mathematical texts contain useful summaries of set theory and Boolean algebra, notably Anton and Kolman [21].

4.1.5 Geometry, trigonometry and topology

Based on the various notations already mentioned above, there is a well-developed notation of geometry and trigonometry for the representation of systems on a plane or in space. In a sense, geometry does not therefore represent a new notation, but there are many special applications of the existing notation, particularly related to the ways in which movement in time and space can be represented on a plane, or in some reduced number of dimensions. This is perhaps the most difficult notation for the beginner to learn and it represents a substantial part of the whole subject of mathematics as it is currently taught in universities.

A special branch of geometry is concerned with ways in which figures are 'connected' rather than with their shape or size. This special branch called topology is thus concerned with the geometrical factors that remain unchanged when an object undergoes a continuous deformation (for example by bending, stretching, or twisting) without tearing or breaking. The notation of topology has led to an elegant development of a theory of catastrophes which is likely to be of increasing importance in the modelling of ecological systems. Some facility and understanding of topological notation, therefore, is desirable [22, 23].

4.2 Families of mathematical models

It should not be imagined that every model has to begin from scratch. It is true that modelling should always begin from a clear statement of the objectives and of the goals of the research of which the modelling forms a part. However, one of the added benefits of the use of mathematical models is that an experienced mathematician can recognize 'families' of models, in much the same way than an experienced botanist is often able to place a plant into a genus even when he does not know the species. It would be impractical, in an outline of this kind, to include all the possible families, and the account in this chapter of the model families will be confined to those which most modellers are likely to encounter, namely:

1. Dynamic models.
2. Matrix models.

3. Stochastic models.
4. Multivariate models.
5. Optimization models.
6. Game theory models.
7. Catastrophe theory models.

This list is far from being exhaustive, and the categories are also not mutually exclusive. The list is, however, sufficient to provide us with some examples of mathematical models applied to real problems, and to illustrate the basic requirements of models in application.

4.2.1 Dynamic models

Dynamic models are based on servo-mechanism theory, itself a relatively recent development, and the use of dynamic models in any practical application depends on the ability of modern high-speed digital computers to solve large numbers (hundreds) of equations in short periods of time. The equations are more or less complex mathematical descriptions of the operation of the system being simulated, and are in the form of expressions for levels of various types which change at rates controlled by decision functions. The level equation may represent accumulations within the system of such variables as weight, number of organisms and energy, and the rate equations govern the change of the levels with time. The decision functions represent the policies or rules, explicit or implicit, which are assumed to control the operation of the system.

Dynamic models of a system can only represent that system to the extent that the equations describing the operation of the components of the model describe accurately the operation of the components of the real system. The popularity of dynamic models arises from the great flexibility of the methods used to describe system operations, including non-linear responses of components to controlling variables, and both positive and negative feedback. This flexibility has some disadvantages, and it is, in any case, usually impossible to include equations for all the components of a system, as the simulation then rapidly becomes too complex. It is, therefore, necessary to obtain an abstraction based on judgement and on assumptions as to which of the many components are those which control the operation of a system.

There is no simple advice that can be given for the construction of a dynamic model of some practical problem. Much depends on the primary skills of the individuals concerned with the task and, particularly, on whether the individuals who have the necessary ecological knowledge also have sufficient mathematical ability to exploit fully the potential of the mathematics. For this reason, dynamic models are often constructed by small teams of research scientists made up of ecologists, mathematicians and resource managers [24–26].

The most convenient start is often a relatively simple word model which can be used as a basis for the sets of system equations which will ultimately define the system. The mathematicians will attempt to formalize the relationships as quickly as possible by equations linking the state variables of the system, while the ecologists and resource managers will attempt to relate these equations to their understanding of the problem, using relational diagrams and re-interpretation of the equations as descriptions with which to compare the original word model. The whole process is an iterative one, going through several cycles of successive approximations. Sometimes, the model will draw heavily upon existing models as parts of the system, e.g. exponential or logistic growth, or will begin as a modification of an existing model. The mathematics acts as a convenient medium for the transfer of experience and also as a medium of communications between the mathematician and the ecologist.

Dynamic models have an intuitive appeal to many ecologists, especially if they also have some reasonable mathematical background. The formulation of the models allows considerable freedom from constraints and assumptions, and allows for the introduction of the non-linearity and feedback which are apparently characteristic of ecological systems. The ecologist is able to mirror or mimic the behaviour of the system as he understands it, and gains some useful insight into the behaviour of the system as a result of changes in the parameters and driving variables. Even where the values of parameters are unknown, relatively simple techniques exist to provide some approximations for these parameters by sequential estimates, or even to use interpolations from turbulated functions. In particularly favourable cases, it may even be possible to test various hypotheses about parameters or functions.

The lack of a formal structure for the models, and the freedom from constraints, can also be a disadvantage. For one thing, the behaviour of even quite simple dynamic models may be very difficult to predict. It requires only one non-linearity and two feedback loops to create a model system whose behaviour will almost certainly be counter-intuitive. As a result, it is desperately easy to construct models whose behaviour, even within the practical limits of the input variables, is unstable or inconsistent with reality. Even more difficult, determination of the way in which systems behave will frequently require extensive and sophisticated experimentation. For example, it is nearly always necessary to test the behaviour of the model in relation to the interaction of changes in two or more input variables, and it is seldom, if ever, sufficient to test the response to changes in one variable at a time.

The inability to predict the behaviour of dynamic models severely limits their value in the development of further theory. Some of the other families of models behave in more predictable ways so that, in exchange for more clearly established assumptions, the responses of the model to changes can be more readily deduced. Admittedly, much of the difficulty in constructing mathematical models is then focused on the testing of the basic assumptions necessary for the use of the model, but this testing will usually be easier, and mathematically more rigorous, than the search for the complex modes of behaviour and discontinuities of dynamic models.

Perhaps the most important disadvantage of dynamic models, however, is the uncertainty of being able to estimate the values of the basic parameters, especially when there are many parameters to be estimated. Although methods are available for deriving estimates of parameters by successive approximation, such methods are usually time-consuming and may be tedious, even on a computer. Furthermore, it is not always possible to arrive at convergent estimates for even relatively simple models, and many of the other families of mathematical models have been specially designed to simplify the estimation of basic parameters, even at the expense of apparent 'reality'. The disadvantage is frequently compounded by the lack of parsimony in the number of relationships, variables, and parameters that is often a feature of dynamic models because of the other praiseworthy desire to mimic reality as closely as possible. For the scientist, it is always necessary to work towards the simplest possible model, so that the entities and relationships are not multiplied needlessly, but this simplicity is not easy to balance against the flexibility of the dynamic models.

Because of their nature and the underlying mathematics of their structure, dynamic models are heavily orientated towards deterministic solutions. Admittedly, stochastic relationships can often be incorporated in such models, but sometimes only with difficulty. As a result, the models of this family do not usually reflect the inherent variability of ecological and biological systems. As will be argued later, it is particularly important to be able to model the variability of ecological systems as well as their average tendencies – indeed, the stability of such systems may depend upon this variability.

To summarize, therefore, dynamic models may well be helpful in the early stages of the systems analysis of a complex ecological problem by concentrating attention on the basic relationships underlying the system and by defining the variables and subsystems that the investigator believes to be critical. In the later stages of the analysis, however, it will often be preferable to switch the main efforts to one of the other families of models.

4.2.2 Matrix models
Dynamic models offer almost complete freedom to the investigator for the expression of those elements considered to be essential to the understanding of the underlying relationships between those variables and entities which are identified in the description of the system. The models usually strive for 'reality' – a recognizable analogy between the mathematics and the physical, chemical or biological processes – sometimes at the expense of mathematical elegance or convenience. The price paid for the 'reality' is frequently the necessity to multiply entities to account for relatively small variations in the behaviour of the system, or difficulty in deriving unbiased valid estimates of the model's parameters. Matrix models represent one family of models in which

'reality' is sacrificed to some extent in order to gain the advantages of the particular mathematical properties of the formulation. The deductive logic of pure mathematics then enables the modeller to examine the consequences of his assumptions without the need for time-consuming 'experimentation' on the model.

One of the earliest forms of matrix model was developed by Lewis [27] and Leslie [28] as a deterministic model predicting the future age structure of a population of female animals from the present known age structure and assumed rates of survival and fecundity. The population is first divided into equal age groups so that the oldest group possible, or the age group in which all the animals surviving die, is known. The model is then represented by a matrix equation in which the numbers of the various animals in the various age classes at times $t + 1$ are obtained by multiplying the numbers of animals in these age classes at time t by a matrix expressing the appropriate fecundity and survival rates for each age class. Repeated application of the model gives predictions in which the latest population is pre-multiplied by the fecundity and survival rates. After some initial instability, the predicted numbers increase exponentially and the numbers of young, middle-aged and old animals maintain a constant ratio to each other. Mathematical analysis of the matrix itself indicates the stable structure of the population without the necessity for time-consuming calculations, repeating the generations of animals. This example illustrates the basic reason for using the more restrictive formulation of the mathematics, in that relatively simple calculation reveals some of the principal properties of the model. This particular example suffers from the same disadvantages as the deterministic exponential model of population growth, in that it assumes that the population size will continue to be increased. A more realistic model can, however, be readily formulated by making all the elements of the matrix functions of some property of population size.

Predator–prey systems, which sometimes show marked oscillations, can also be encompassed by matrix models, by the relatively simple exploitation of the techniques relating population size and survival. Seasonal and random environmental changes and the effects of time lags may be similarly incorporated, although the models necessarily become increasingly complex in formulation. There are many developments of the basic matrix model outlined above. All of these developments represent modifications or additions to the elements of the matrix, and one of the simplest of these is the investigation of the effects of harvesting different parts of the population. Lefkovitch [29], for example, gives a useful introduction to the mathematics of harvesting models which he derived from his original models for immigration. Similarly, the model can be readily extended to include both sexes, and Williamson [30] gives the simple case of a population divided into only three age classes.

Perhaps the best known modifications of matrix models, however, have been concerned with the consideration of size structures or discrete stages within the population. For example, Usher [31–34] has used such models to investigate the management and harvesting of forests, where trees are classified by size as well as age. In contrast, Lefkovitch [29, 35, 36] has applied matrix models to insect pests of stored products, where the structure of the insect populations is defined by the development stages of the insect life cycle.

Dynamic processes such as the cycling of nutrients and the flow of energy in ecosystems can also be modelled by the use of matrices, exploiting the natural compartmentation of the ecosystem into its species composition or into its trophic levels. Losses from the ecosystem are assumed to be the difference between input and some of the output from, and storage in, any one compartment. Finally, an extension of the concept of matrix models occurs in the Markov models discussed in a subsequent section.

Matrix models represent one family of models in which the 'realism' of the model is partly sacrificed in order to obtain the benefit of the mathematical formulation. The same formulation also imposes constraints upon the way in which the models can be used, but these constraints are balanced by the convenience of the computations and by the relative ease of establishing the values of the basic parameters.

Matrix models, therefore, represent an important, and neglected, family of models in ecology. So far, this family has been relatively unexploited in the ecological sciences, and only a few research workers have published applications of such models. In part, the unfamiliarity of biologists and ecologists with matrix algebra may have been responsible for the neglect of matrix models, although the differential and difference equations of dynamic models perhaps make an even greater demand on the mathematical ability of the modeller.

4.2.3 Stochastic models

The families of models which we have so far considered have all been deterministic. That is to say, from a given starting point, the outcome of the model's response is necessarily the same and is predicted by the mathematical relationships incorporated by the model. Deterministic models are the logical development of the kinds of mathematics we learn early in our mathematics courses, and particularly in what has come to be called 'applied mathematics', i.e. mathematics applied to physics. Such models are necessarily mathematical analogues of physical processes in which there is a one-to-one correspondence between cause and effect. There is, however, a later development of mathematics which enables relationships to be expressed in terms of probabilities, and in which the outcome of a model's response is not certain. Models which incorporate probabilities are known as stochastic models and such models are particularly valuable in simulating the variability and complexity of ecological systems. Probabilities can, of course, be introduced into almost any kind of model, for example in dynamic models, and particularly in the study of the stability of such models to variations in the basic parameters.

(a) Distribution models One of the simplest applications of stochastic models to ecological problems is in the mapping of spatial patterns of living organisms. There is, of course, a wide range of statistical distributions capable of describing spatial patterns. The problem arises from the frequent need in ecology to understand and to predict the numbers of organisms which will be found on some defined areas, or on some equally well-defined unit, for example a single plant, a single leaf or a single seed. In general, we will not know the average density of the organisms, and we therefore need a mathematical model which will provide us with an efficient measure of the average number of occurrences and which will also provide us with a measure of the variability of the occurrences and the pattern of this variability.

Ignoring the practical possibility of a totally uniform distribution, i.e. that each sampling unit has exactly the same number of individuals, with no variation, the simplest hypothesis is that each organism has a constant, but unknown, probability of occurring in the unit and that the presence of the individual has no effect upon its neighbours, or, in other words, that the probabilities of the occurrences of individuals are independent.

The resulting distribution is that of the Poisson distribution, in which the average number of individuals per sampling unit also equals the variance of the number of individuals from unit to unit. Tests of the adequacy of the Poisson distribution to describe the spatial distribution of the organisms, and hence the hypothesis that the probability of occurrence of an individual is constant and not affected by the presence of other individuals, can be made either by comparing the observed frequency of occurrences with the frequency that would be expected from the theoretical distribution, or by comparing the mean and the variance of the observed frequencies.

If the hypothesis of the Poisson distribution is rejected, some alternative hypotheses may be formulated about the distribution. Formulation will inevitably be guided by what is known about the organisms, and, since there is always an infinity of possible hypotheses, the search for an adequate mathematical model should be consistent with the ecology of the problem, rather than with the convenience of the mathematics. On the other hand, the model should not be over-elaborate, or require more parameters than can be estimated from any reasonable set of data. Many of the alternatives to the Poisson distribution provide models for quite specific departures from randomness, and their appropriateness therefore depends on the underlying ecology.

If the individual organisms move away from each other, especially as the number of individuals increases, the characteristic feature of the distribution will be its regularity and the uniform spacing of the individuals, with the variance of the number of individuals becoming smaller than the mean number of individuals. Territorial behaviour of animals, for example, will often produce a relative uniform spacing.

The dispersion of sedentary invertebrates may also be regular over a small area of stream or lake bottom. A regular distribution of this kind may be approximated by the positive binomial distribution for which the expected frequency distribution is given by the expansion of:

$$n(q+p)^k$$

where n is the number of sampling units, p the probability of any point in the sampling unit, $q = 1 - p$, and k is the maximum possible number of individuals a sampling unit could retain.

In practice, estimates of the parameters k, p and q are obtained from samples of the population. A test of the conformity of observed counts with a positive binomial distribution is again provided by a comparison of the observed and expected frequencies, using a chi-square test of goodness of fit.

Where the spatial distribution of individuals is neither random nor regular, and the variance of the numbers of individuals per sample unit is greater than the mean number of individuals per unit, the distribution is usually referred to as 'contagious', indicating that there are clumps or patches of individuals and irregular gaps with no individuals. There are, of course, many environmental factors which can contribute to uneven distributions of individuals, and there is frequently a tendency for some species to aggregate and thus produce clumping even without the influence of environmental factors. The resulting pattern of distribution is dependent upon the size of the groups, the distance between the groups, spatial distribution of the groups, and the spatial distribution of individuals within groups.

Several mathematical models have been suggested for such irregular distributions, but a complete list of these distributions is outside the scope of this outline. It is sufficient to indicate that appropriate distributions exist for most of the ecological circumstances which are likely to be encountered. As the number of organisms per sample unit increases, or, alternatively, as the number of sample units increases, all of these distributions approach closer and closer to the Normal distribution which is fundamental to many of the basic ideas and tests of statistical mathematics. Even for quite small numbers of samples, approximation to the Normal distribution can be achieved by relatively simple transformations of the observed counts, and the identification of the correct transformation may itself provide an adequate guide to the distribution of the organisms. Alternative methods of investigating spatial distributions have also been developed from measurements of the distances between neighbouring individuals. Again, these methods are outside the scope of this outline, but Pielou [37] and Greig-Smith [38] summarize some of the earlier techniques.

(b) Analysis of variance models One of the most widely used stochastic models in scientific research is the one which underlies the statistical technique of analysis of variance, although many scientists who use

statistical methods are scarcely aware that they are using a model, perhaps because this aspect of the analysis is seldom emphasized in elementary statistical texts. Nevertheless, the linear and factorial models underlying the analysis of variance have been of considerable importance in the development of science, and will probably remain important, despite the limitations of their basic assumptions. The development of these models has been one of the major achievements of the last 50 years, and an example is given in Model 11. These techniques are extraordinarily powerful, despite the apparent limitations of the basic assumptions which are:

1. The effects are assumed to be additive.
2. The residual effects are assumed to be independent from observation to observation and to be distributed with zero mean and the same variance.
3. If tests of significance and estimated confidence limits are required, the residuals are assumed to be Normally distributed.

Even when these assumptions can be regarded as only approximately true, or where the data have to be transformed to make the assumptions approximately true, the analysis of variance provides a method of constructing models of ecological populations, and of estimating the parameters of the models from sample observations. The models can be complex and contain linear and higher order interactions of many

Model 11 Analysis of variance model for sampling blanket bog vegetation

Analysis of variance

Source of variation	Degrees of freedom	Sum of squares	Mean square
Plots	1	10 788.9	10 788.9
Quadrats within plots	8	8 581.8	1 072.7
Sub-samples within quadrats	10	2 752.8	275.3
Total	19	22 123.3	

Variance components

	Mean square is an estimate of
Plots	$\sigma^2 + 2\sigma_q^2 + 10\sigma_p^2$
Quadrats	$\sigma^2 + 2\sigma_q^2$
Sub-samples	σ^2

Estimate of variance due to quadrats =
$$S_q^2 = (1072.7 - 275.3)/2 = 398.7$$
Estimate of variance due to plots =
$$S_p^2 = (10\ 788.9 - 1072.7)/10 = 971.6$$
Variance of plot mean based on k plots, n quadrats, and m sub-samples
$$(S_{\bar{p}})^2 = (1/d)[S^2 + nS_p^2 + nmS],$$
where $d = k.n.m$.

44

factors. For example, by carefully designed experiments and subsequent analysis, it is possible to test the effects of several different elements in fertilizer treatments, and simultaneously test whether the effects of each element are the same in the presence or absence of any or all of the other elements. Similarly, again by carefully designed experiments and the use of factorial models, the extent to which the management of an ecological system requires to be modified to take account of annual changes in climate can be determined. The development of such models, however, is outside the scope of this outline.

(c) Regression models The linear models of the analysis of variance are a special case of the more general regression models carried by the expression:

$$y = \beta_0 + \beta_1 x_1 + \beta_2 x_2 + \ldots \beta_p x_p.$$

In this expression, y is assumed to be a random variable distributed about a mean that is dependent on the values of the p variables $x_1 \ldots x_p$. It is assumed that these variables affect only the mean y, and, in particular, that the variance is constant. Where tests of significance are required, it is further assumed that y is Normally distributed about this mean. Finally, it is assumed that the mean can be regarded as a linear function of the x variables, although there can also be functional relationships between the xs, so that polynomial and other non-linear functions are included in these more general models. As in the special case of the additive of model experimental designs, the parameters of the model are usually estimated by minimizing the residual sum of squares for a sample from a defined population. Sprent [39] gives a valuable discussion of the uses of models in regression, and advice and programs for the fitting of regression models to actual data are given by Davies [6]. Model 2 has already provided an example of this type.

(d) Markov models Markov models are a hybrid between the matrix models discussed in Section 4.2.2 and the stochastic models discussed in the last sections. In these models, the basic format is of the matrix of entries expressing the probabilities of the transition from one state to another at a specified time step. The model is, therefore, exactly similar to those of the matrix models, except that all of the probabilities in the columns add to one.

A first-order Markov model is one in which the future development of a system is determined by the present state of the system and is independent of the way in which that state has developed. The sequence of results generated by such a model is often termed a Markov chain.

The potential value of Markov models is particularly great where ecological systems under study exhibit Markovian properties, and especially those of a stationary, first-order Markov chain, where several interesting and important analyses of the model can be made. For example:

1. Algebraic analysis of the transition matrix will determine the existence of transient sets of states, closed sets of states, or an absorbing state. Further analysis enables the basic transition matrix to be partitioned and several components investigated separately, thus simplifying the ecological system being studied.
2. Analysis of the transition matrix can also lead to the calculation of the mean times to move from one state to another and the mean length of stay in a particular state once it is entered.
3. Where closed or absorbing states exist, the probability of absorption and the mean time to absorption can be calculated.

The choice between Markov and other models often depends upon the objectives of the study, but, when a straightforward Markovian approach can be used, the possibilities of further algebraic analysis, leading to a better appreciation of the stochastic character of many ecological processes, as well as to the calculation of mean passage times, time to absorption and the degree of stability and convergence within the defined state, provide additional information of direct ecological and management value.

4.2.4 Multivariate models

A statistician makes a distinction between 'variables' and 'variates'. The term 'variable' is used for any quantity which takes different values for different individuals, or different values for the same individual at different times. The statistical definition of the term, therefore, is of a quantity which may take any one of a specified set of values, and these values may be continuous, as in measurements of height or weight, or discontinuous, as in counts of individuals. Indeed, in some instances, it is convenient to use the word to denote non-measurable characteristics. For example, 'sex' may be regarded as a variable in this sense, as any individual may take one of two values, 'male' or 'female'.

A 'variate' is a quantity which may take any one of the values of a specified set with a specified relative frequency or probability. Such variates are sometimes also known as random variables and they are to be regarded as defined, not merely by a set of permissible values like any ordinary mathematical variable, but by an associated frequency or probability function expressing how often these values appear in the application under discussion. There are many situations in ecology where models have to capture the behaviour of more than one variate; these models are known collectively as 'multivariate' and are related to techniques known collectively as 'multivariate analysis', an expression which is used rather loosely to denote the analysis of data which are multivariate in the sense that each individual bears the values of p variates. Broadly, multivariate models may be divided into two main categories, i.e. those in which some variates are used to predict others, and those in which all the variates are of the same kind, and no attempt is made to predict one set from the other. For the latter, which may be broadly described as descriptive models, there is a further subdivision into those models in which all the inputs are qualitative and which include principal component analysis and cluster analysis, and those models for which some at least of the inputs are qualitative rather than quantitative. For the latter, the reciprocal averaging model is the more appropriate. Predictive models, on the other hand, may first be divided according to the number of variates predicted, and then by whether or not all the predictors are quantitative. Where several variates are predicted, the model of canonical analysis is the most appropriate; where only one variate is predicted and there are two *a priori* groups of individuals, the model of discriminant analysis is the most appropriate of the available models, while, where there are more than two *a priori* groups of individuals, canonical variate analysis will provide the most useful approach [55].

(a) Principal component analysis Principal component analysis is probably the best known of the multivariate models, and is certainly one of the simplest ways of studying multivariate variation. It is a technique which can be applied to all data which satisfy the following basic requirements:

1. For each of a number of individual sampling units, the same variables are measured and recorded. All the measurements must be made on each individual, and any individuals for which the measurements are incomplete should be eliminated from the analysis, unless some suitable technique for replacing the missing values is found.
2. The variables selected for analysis are assumed to be continuous, or, if discrete, to increase by sufficiently small intervals of measurement as to be regarded as approximately continuous. It is possible that the analysis can be extended to deal with qualitative attributes which are scaled or scored, but only by weakening some of the basic assumptions, and alternative methods of analysis are therefore preferable.
3. No attempt should be made to add ratios or linear functions of the original variables to those to be included in the analysis, or to replace any of the originally measured variables by ratios or linear functions.

The objectives of a principal component analysis may include one or more of the following:

1. Examination of the correlations between the separate variables.
2. Reduction of the basic dimensions of the variability expressed by the individual sampling units to the smallest number of meaningful dimensions.
3. Elimination of variables which contribute relatively little extra information to the study.
4. Examination of the most informative groupings of the individual sampling units, or the implication of some *a priori* structure imposed upon the sampling units.

47

5. Determination of the objective weighting of the variables in the construction of indices of variation.
6. Identification of individual sampling units of doubtful or unknown origin.
7. The recognition of misidentified sample units.

Not all of these objectives will be of equal importance in any particular study, and some may be entirely absent. Nevertheless, the method provides one possible solution to such problems.

In essence, principal component analysis involves the extraction of eigenvalues and eigenvectors of the matrix of the correlation coefficients of the original variables. The resulting eigenvalues and eigenvectors define the components of total variability described by the original variables as linear functions of these variables, with coefficients so chosen that the functions are mathematically independent, or orthogonal, to each other. There is no necessity that the components have any valid ecological interpretation, but practical experience with the techniques suggests that a valid interpretation may often be expected for those components which account for a significant part of the total variation. Furthermore, the calculation of the value of these components for each of the individuals included in the study provides a ready way of summarizing the essential variation of the individuals, examining their relationships with each other, and identifying a form of transformation of the original data so as to derive a more readily understood model. Model 12 gives an example of principal component analysis.

(b) Cluster analysis An alternative multivariate model, when all inputs are quantitative, is that of cluster analysis. Cluster analysis encompasses many diverse techniques for discovering structure within complex bodies of data. In a typical example, and as in principal component analysis, the data base consists of a sample of units each described by a series of selective variables. The objective is to group either the data units, or the variables, into clusters so that the elements within a cluster have a high degree of natural association amongst themselves, while the clusters are relatively distinct from one another. The approach to the problem and the results achieved depend principally on how the investigator chooses to give operational meaning to the phrases 'natural association' and 'relatively distinct'.

In general, cluster analysis assumes that little or nothing is known about the structure which underlies the data set. All that is available is the collection of observations whose structure is unknown. The operational objective in this case is to discover a category structure which fits the observations, and the problem is frequently stated as one of finding 'natural groups'. The essence of cluster analysis might equally be viewed as that of assigning appropriate meanings to the terms 'natural groups' and 'natural associations'. Cluster analysis is the attempt to group sample points in multidimensional space into separate sets which,

Variable		Mean	Standard deviation
1	Cs-137 0–15 cm	13.1	5.28
2	Cs-137 0–30 cm	17.6	6.36
3	Pu-238 + 240 0–15 cm	0.295	0.136
4	Pu-238 0–15 cm	0.013	0.0073
5	Gamma radiation	13.8	4.12

1			Correlation coefficients	
0.947	2			
0.461	0.465	3		
0.326	0.386	0.749	4	
0.467	0.523	0.354	0.230	5

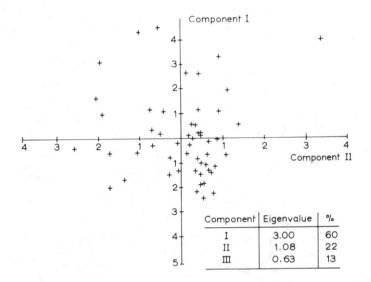

Component	Eigenvalue	%
I	3.00	60
II	1.08	22
III	0.63	13

Model 12 Principal component analysis of radionuclide depositions in Cumbria

it is hoped, will correspond to observed features of the sample. The group of points may themselves be grouped into larger sets, so that all the points are eventually classified hierarchically. This hierarchical classification can be represented diagrammatically, and it is usual to incorporate a scale into such a diagram to indicate the degree of similarity of the various groups. An example of a cluster analysis dendrogram is given in Model 13.

Many techniques for cluster analysis have been developed during recent years and many of these techniques have shortcomings and limitations in their use in practice. In general, some caution should be used in attempting cluster analysis of data, and methods should be based on a well-defined mathematical formulation of the problem. The growing tendency to regard classification and cluster analysis as a satisfactory alternative to clear thinking needs to be condemned, and other ways of summarizing data may often be suggested as alternatives to cluster analysis and classification itself. Nevertheless, when cluster

49

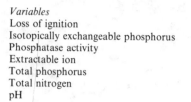

Variables
Loss of ignition
Isotopically exchangeable phosphorus
Phosphatase activity   25 soils
Extractable ion
Total phosphorus
Total nitrogen
pH

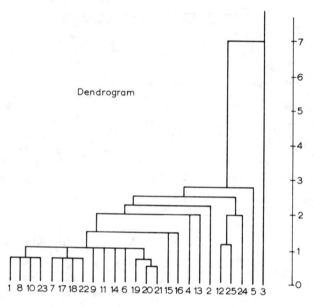

Dendrogram

1 8 10 23 7 17 18 22 9 11 14 6 19 20 21 15 16 4 13 2 12 25 24 5 3

Model 13 Cluster analysis of Lake District soils

analysis is used as only one of the models of an analysis, the results may be revealing and helpful [40].

(c) Reciprocal averaging and association analysis Where some of the variates in descriptive models are qualitative, principal component analysis is of less value. Cluster analysis can still be used, even on wholly qualitative data, by devising indices of similarity which are then translated into distances by formulae. However, there are some specially devised multivariate models for qualitative data, and two of the most valuable of these are those of reciprocal averaging and association analysis. These models are especially appropriate for presence/absence data which are commonly found in ecology, as in the recording of the presence or absence of particular species in quadrats. Geometrically, these data can be regarded as a set of points situated at the vertices of a hypercube, for which the ordination does not depend on the explicit use of the distances between the vertices [56].

50

(d) Discriminant function If we now turn to the broadly predictive models, it is necessary to make a distinction between models for which only one variate is predicted from two or more variables, and those for which several variates are predicted from two or more other variables. Multiple regression analysis, which has already been cited as an example of linear stochastic models, is one type of predictive model which enables the value of one variate to be predicted from the values of two or more variables, usually known as regressor variables. Where the regressor variables are, in fact, variates, i.e. variables with a specified relative frequency or probability, it can be shown that, mathematically, the estimation procedures are equivalent, even when there is a mixture of regressor variates and regressor variables in the one model. Thus, in practice, there is usually little to worry about with classical regression models for variates, variables, or a mixture of both, providing that they are reasonably error-free measurements of what they are supposed to measure.

In predicting one variate, however, there is a classical model of discrimination for which the basic theory has been known for over 40 years. In considering this theory, it is useful to distinguish between a model providing a discrimination between two groups, and known as the discriminant function, and a model providing a discrimination between more than two groups, and known as canonical variates.

Fisher's [41] classical model of the discriminant function deals with the problem of how best to discriminate between two *a priori* groups, each individual of which has been measured in respect of several variables. The model provides a linear function of the measurements on each variable such that an individual can be assigned to one or other of the two groups with the least chance of being misclassified. The discriminant function is writen as:

$$z = \mathbf{a}_1 x_1 + \mathbf{a}_2 x_2 + \ldots \mathbf{a}_n x_n$$

where **a** is the vector of discriminant coefficients and the vector of observations or measurements made on an individual which is to be assigned to one or other of the two groups. For this model, we are only considering the possibility of two groups, and, while we may decide that some individual cannot be assigned with any confidence to one of the groups, we are not considering the formation of further groups.

The discriminant function provides a powerful and practical model for discriminating between two *a priori* groups. There are many ecological situations, however, in which we wish to discriminate between more than two groups. In the simplest of such situations, a third group may be formed by the hybrids between the two original groups. Even in taxonomic research, however, considerably more complex problems may be encountered, as in the study of grasshoppers by Blackith and Blackith [42] and in the studies of the ecology of insects living on broom plants by Waloff [43].

The multivariate model of canonical variate analysis is a powerful and extremely flexible tool for the investigation of the ability to discriminate between several *a priori* groups, and is a logical extension of the discriminant function. An example is given in Model 14.

(e) Canonical correlation The multivariate model appropriate to one of the most difficult of all statistical problems is that defining the relationships between two or more sets of variates. As an alternative to the assumption of an *a priori* structure imposed on the individuals, or rows, of the basic data matrix, we now assume that the variates, or columns, of the matrix can be divided into two sets, with r and q variates in each set, so that $P = r + q$.

The multivariate model of canonical correlation provides a powerful technique for summarizing and exploring complex relationships between two sets of variables. It is a model which has been neglected, mainly because of difficulties in computation. Efficient algorithms for these computations are now readily available, however, so that there is

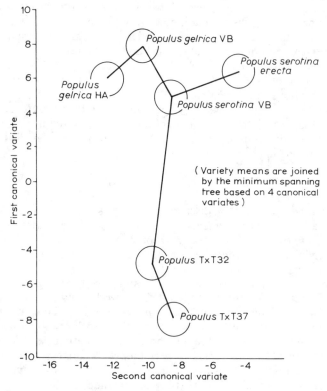

Model 14 Canonical variate model of the taxonomic differences between some varieties of poplars

Model 15 Canonical correlation model of the physical environment and invertebrates of Morecambe Bay

Eigenvalues and canonical correlations

| | | | Proportion of variance | |
| | | Canonical | | |
Number	Eigenvalue	correlation	Species	Environment
1	0.313	0.559	0.25	0.24
2	0.112	0.334	0.13	0.18
3	0.080	0.283	0.16	0.19

Scaled vectors for species

| | Scaled vectors for correlation | | |
Species	1	2	3
Macoma balthica	1.000	−0.326	−0.230
Tellina tenuis	−0.067	−0.431	0.016
Hydrobia ulvae	0.012	−0.474	−0.674
Corophium volutator	0.146	1.000	−1.000
Nereis diversicolor	0.194	0.007	0.725
Arenicola marina	0.067	0.786	0.964
Nephthys hombergii	0.007	−0.910	−0.099

Scaled vectors for environment

| | Scaled vectors for correlation | | |
Environmental variables	1	2	3
% particles > 250 μm	0.060	0.253	0.104
% particles 126–250 μm	0.913	0.765	−0.616
% particles 62.5–125 μm	1.000	0.720	−0.997
% particles < 62.5 μm	0.666	1.000	−1.000
% loss of ignition at 550°C	0.015	−0.126	0.124
% calcium	0.052	0.105	0.039
% phosphorus	−0.005	0.062	0.174
% nitrogen	0.936	−0.023	0.160

little excuse for continuing neglect. An example is given in Model 15.

The multivariate models exploit the mathematical properties of matrices of observations and take account of the inherent structure and partitioning of these matrices. As in some of the other mathematical models, we have exchanged the freedom of dynamic simulation for the knowledge of the properties and behaviour of certain types of mathematics. The constraints are balanced by a surer insight into the logic of the model as an approximation to reality.

4.2.5 *Optimization models*

An important range of models, developed during and since the 1939–1945 World War, is that of the method of mathematical programming. These models may be described as 'optimization' models, in the sense that they are used to find the maximum or minimum of some mathematical expression or function by setting values to certain variables which we are free to alter within defined limits. Of course, nearly all models can be used to search for either an optimum or minimum. Whether or not this is a sensible use of the model will depend entirely upon the context of the problem, but there will be many occasions on which it is necessary to explore the possibility of being able to increase the output of some ecological system by modifying its environment or by altering the methods of management. It is, indeed, one of the main reasons for the use of models that we should be able to look at the consequences of such changes.

In this situation, it is possible to formulate models so that the search for the optimum combination of the critical values is facilitated, and the underlying mathematics of this formulation was developed quite independently in the early application of mathematical techniques to practical problems that has now come to be known as 'operational research' or, in North America, as 'operations research'. Even more confusingly, the general class of solutions was known as 'mathematical programming' before the word 'programming' was adopted for the writing of instructions for computers. The fact that most mathematical programming is now closely associated with computers only adds to the confusion.

(a) Linear programming The simplest form of mathematical programming is that of 'linear' programming. In this model, we begin with a linear objective function:

$$Y = a_1 x_1 + a_2 x_2 + \ldots + a_n x_n = \Sigma a_i x_i$$

and we wish to make this function a maximum or a minimum subject to one or more constraints which are also expressed as linear functions, although, initially, these constraints may be inequalities, e.g.:

$$b_i x_i + b_3 x_3 \gtrless Z.$$

Frequently, there are implicit constraints that the x_i cannot be negative.

When there are only two variables, optimization problems of this kind can be solved by graphical methods rather simply. For more than two variables, the problem rapidly becomes more difficult and the usual approach to the solution is by what is known as the 'Simplex' method. In essence, the inequalities in the constraints are first removed by introducing some additional 'slack' variables. Any feasible solution to the problem is then sought, and, once such a solution has been found, iterative attempts are made to 'improve' the solution, i.e. move it closer to the defined optimum of the objective function by making small

54

Maximize the function
$$Z = 25x_1 + 30x_2 \text{ Joules}$$
Subject to the constraints
$$2x_1 + 3x_2 \leqslant 120 \text{ Joules}$$
$$2x_1 + x_2 \leqslant 80 \text{ Joules}$$
$$x_1 \geqslant 0$$
$$x_2 \geqslant 0$$
Maximum is given by $x_1 = 30$, $x_2 = 20$ so that
$$Z = 25(30) + 30(20) = 1350 \text{ Joules}$$

Model 16 Optimum predator strategies by linear programming (see Chaston [54])

changes in the values of the variables. This iterative procedure continues until no further improvement can be made.

One of the advantages of optimization models is that they always illuminate two important facets of the problem. The solution gives the value of the variables of the objective function necessary for that function to be either a maximum or a minimum, depending on how the problem was defined. However, the method also indicates the constraint which needs to be relaxed for the optimum value of the objective function to be improved. In this way, the experimenter can examine more carefully his definition of the problem and, in particular, his estimates of the coefficients of the variables in the objective function and the nature of the constraint. If he finds that the estimates can be improved, or the constraint relaxed, he may be able to find an even better solution.

A graphical method of solution can usually be employed only when there are two variables in the objective function and the constraints, although such solutions can often be found when there are several constraints. However, well-defined algorithms exist for the solutions of linear programming problems. A simple example is given in Model 16.

(b) Non-linear programming Useful though linear programming may be, it is easy to see that many problems will be difficult (or impossible) to express in terms of linear objective functions and constraints. Indeed, non-linearity in either the objective function or the constraints, or both, introduces quite disproportionate levels of difficulty in finding appropriate solutions. So, too, do problem formulations which impose limitations on the size of the lumps in which units of some particular resource can be allocated. There is, therefore, a well-developed theory of non-linear programming, although relatively few ecological models have drawn heavily upon this theory. Van Dyne *et al.* [44] have summarized a few of the important recent uses, and have introduced some potential needs, of optimization techniques in natural resource management.

(c) Dynamic programming Some large optimization problems can be reformulated as a series of smaller problems, arranged in sequences of

55

time or space, or both. A reformulation of this kind is frequently desirable in order to reduce the computational effort of finding a solution, although care has to be taken to ensure that the sum of the optimal solutions of the problems approaches the optimum solution of the whole problem. This search for the best solution at each of a number of stages is known as 'dynamic programming'. The mathematics of the models is frequently complex, and, for this reason, there are relatively few examples of successful examples in ecology.

Interested readers who want to learn more about optimization will find the book by Converse [45] a useful introduction. In addition to a broad study of the theory of optimization, the book contains some excellent general-purpose computer programs in BASIC.

4.2.6 Game theory models

Closely related to mathematical programming models are the models which are based on the theory of games. The simplest of these models is known as the two-person zero-sum game. Such games are characterized by having two sets of interests represented, one of which may be nature or some other external force, and by being 'closed', in the sense that what one player loses in the game the other must win. The theory can be extended to many-person non-zero-sum games, but the extension is well outside the scope of this introductory outline.

Williams [46] gives an excellent introduction to game theory, written in an interesting and humorous way with a wealth of practical examples. Game theory models represent an interesting and so-far little explored alternative approach to the solution of strategic problems. The extension to the more complex non-zero-sum games and to many-person games in which coalitions can be formed between the players represents a field of research which deserves increased attention, particularly in ecological research related to the assessment of environmental impact and environmental planning.

4.2.7 Catastrophe theory models

The theory of catastrophe is an elegant development of mathematical topology applied to systems which have four basic properties, namely bimodality, discontinuity, hysteresis and divergence.

The elementary cusp catastrophe is illustrated in Model 17. This system is assumed to be represented by a variable x which is dependent upon two variables p and q. Because of the fold in the surface representing the dependence of x on p and q, the behaviour of the system varies according to the values of p and q. If, for example, p goes from P_1 to P_2, the system moves from A until it encounters the singularity and then makes a catastrophic jump to the lower surface before moving to B. If the system moves from C to D, however, a similar change in the value of p does not encounter the singularity. Whether or not the singularity is encountered depends on the relative values of both p and q.

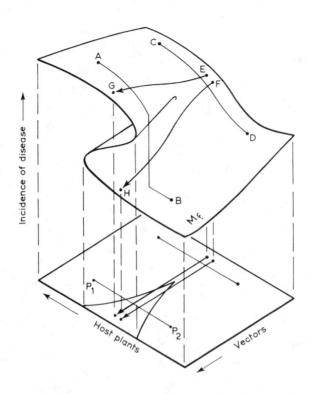

Model 17 Cusp catastrophe model of plant disease carried by an insect vector

Model 17 also illustrates divergence in a cusp catastrophe, where the system is shown in two nearby states E and F. If the value of q is reduced, the system moves steadily to the points G and H respectively. Even though both paths start arbitrarily close, and both experience the same change in the parameter q, they end at widely separated final states. Because of the existence of the cusp, the paths of the two changes diverge, that of EG ending on the upper sheet of the manifold, and that of FH ending on the lower sheet of the manifold.

A simple, but comprehensive, introduction to the application of catastrophe theory to ecological systems is given by Jones [47]. A fuller account is given by Poston and Stewart [22].

Catastrophe theory models have attracted a lot of interest and attention since they were first proposed in 1970. The models have considerable intellectual and visual appeal, but are not easy to apply to highly multivariate situations. There are also serious difficulties to be overcome in estimating the parameters of manifolds from ecological data.

5 Do I need a computer?

5.1 Access to computers

Even within a few years, access to electronic computers has changed dramatically. Ten years ago, even if you had computer facilities close to where you lived or worked, access to those facilities would have been by leaving a batch of punched cards or a reel of punched paper tape on a desk in the computer department. Some time later, you would have received a pile of computer output, and perhaps some new cards or a new tape, together with your original cards or tape. If you were lucky, or very skilful, one of four runs on the computer would have achieved what you set out to do. The others would have been abortive because the operator did not understand your instructions, your program was incorrect, there was something wrong with your data, or some combination of all three. Under the most favourable conditions, you could have counted on about one successful run a day.

Now, your access to even the largest computer is likely to be through some kind of terminal. This may be a machine like a typewriter, providing you with a written copy of what you have done, or it may be a visual display terminal with a small cathode ray tube screen on which what you have typed is displayed, together with the response from the computer. A large quantity of results will probably still be printed on a fast line-printer or on some kind of plotter for you to collect later. The important point, however, is that your use of the computer is interactive. If something quite trivial prevents your program from working, you have an opportunity to correct the error. You can guide the computer through a complex set of decisions about the form of analysis to be done, in response to the results of intermediate calculations as they are printed or displayed on your terminal. Used in this way, it is possible to get tens, or even hundreds, of successful runs on any one day.

Today's micro-computers are quite capable of controlling several terminals, and may themselves act as 'intelligent terminals' to much larger main-frame computers. Quite small tasks will then be done on the micro-computer, but any task requiring larger facilities than can be provided locally will be sent automatically to the main-frame machine. The main-frame computer may itself pass the task to another computer along a network of large computers. All of this activity, however, will take place without your knowledge. All that you will be aware of is the ability to do large amounts of work relatively easily, provided that you have a very clear understanding of exactly what it is that you want to do – something that is easier said than done!

However, by far the most exciting development of the last few years has been that of the new micro-processors. For a few hundreds of pounds, it is now possible to buy computers with capabilities that we could only imagine even a few short years ago. A machine little bigger than a typewriter is now capable of doing more than machines which filled whole rooms with equipment, and which required elaborate air-conditioning and safety systems. The rapid growth of the home computer industry seems likely to transform totally our attitudes towards computation and modelling, as well as those towards the storage and use of data of all kinds. Even today, the really serious modeller will almost certainly have acquired one of these machines for his personal use, and will be able to turn to the machine whenever he has a spare moment to progress with the task he has in hand. One of the principal attractions of working with a computer in this way is that the intermediate stages of any task can be held in the computer, ready for retrieval as soon as there is time to continue, thus making it possible to proceed whenever the opportunity occurs or when the modeller has the necessary inspiration to overcome his latest difficulty.

5.2 Computer languages

The new computer user will usually be advised to use the computer through the medium of one or more special 'package' programs. These are sets of special instructions to the computer, known as 'programs', to enable it to perform a limited range of well-defined functions. Computer scientists often devote a considerable amount of thought and energy to the development of special 'packages' for a wide variety of computer applications, including modelling. The aim is to bring modelling with the aid of the computer within the capability of someone who wants to use the computer without much understanding of how a computer works or how to write programs for himself. Computer scientists often make the point that it should not be necessary for everyone to 're-invent the wheel' each time they use the computer. There will be plenty of people, therefore, anxious to persuade you that all you need for modelling on a computer is contained in this or that 'package'.

Regrettably, perhaps, these assurances have not been fulfilled, and are unlikely ever to be fulfilled. Unless you are content to tread only on very well-worn paths in the development of models, you will quickly find that any 'package' you are using does not have some highly desirable feature for the solution of the particular problems with which you are concerned. As a result, you will be constrained by the contents of the package rather than by the mathematics or logic of the model, and life is difficult enough without having additional constraints imposed on it. You may even find, as you gain more experience, that some parts of the package actually give you results which are incorrect. Many of the people who write 'package' programs are not really experts in the disciplines necessary for the correct use of computers. Beware, especially, of most of the package programs for statistical analysis which you will almost certainly encounter during your analysis and exploration of the models that you build.

An alternative approach to modelling on computers is through the use of special-purpose languages for modelling. These differ from the package programs in that they offer a more flexible language in which the problem to be solved can be expressed and then computed through the use of subroutines or 'macros' contained within the language. Several such languages exist, especially on large computer systems, some of the best known being CSMP, SIMULA, and DYNAMO. Certainly, the greater flexibility of these languages makes them much more attractive than the packages, unless you are content to use highly standardized approaches to the solution of your problems. Nevertheless, you will ultimately encounter a situation in which the specialized language no longer caters for your particular requirements, forcing you to learn another special-purpose language which contains the facilities you require. The alternative is for you to confine yourself to problems which can be solved within the constraints of the languages you have learnt.

Package programs and special-purpose modelling languages are intended to make the use of computers available to people who have not learnt how to program the computers for themselves. In the early days of the use of computers, there was some point in trying to make access to computers easier. Computer languages were difficult to learn and to use, and each computer had its own special language. Writing programs was a time-consuming business, and was fraught with all kinds of problems – not least that of deciding exactly what the computer was expected to do. Since that time, however, there has been a steady development of computer languages themselves. Indeed, a study of this development of the ways in which computers can be programmed is one of the most interesting facets of recent scientific history [48].

Most programming today is done in one of the many so-called high-level languages, and especially in BASIC, FORTRAN, or ALGOL. New languages are constantly being developed, and languages like APL, PASCAL, and COMAL are now becoming readily available on even the smallest micro-computers. These languages are not difficult to learn. BASIC can be learnt by almost anyone within two or three days, and the effort to become reasonably proficient in the use of a computer language is about equivalent to that required to learn to drive a car. There is therefore very little excuse for anyone not learning to write their own programs, or to make use of the immense library of algorithms and subroutines available to the user who can work directly in one or more of the high-level languages.

The best advice I can give anyone who wants to model seriously is to learn at least one of the more commonly used high-level languages. The various experts tend to disagree about which of the languages is 'best' – a fair indication that there probably is no such thing as 'best'! BASIC is probably the easiest to learn from scratch, and is readily available on most computers, from the largest main-frames to the smallest micros. If you are not sure which language to learn, try several, and then concentrate on the one which appeals to you most and for which you have available facilities. There is no need to take too much notice of the experts; they are mostly concerned with persuading you to use the language they have developed themselves, or the one they use. Good introductions to BASIC are given by Kemeny and Kurtz [49], Sanderson [50] and Alcock [51].

The point to be emphasized is that, by learning to program the computer yourself, you can begin to model without being constrained by what someone else thinks should be available to you. It doesn't matter if, occasionally, you re-invent the wheel if, in the process, you discover for yourself the principle which underlies the wheel. In time, you will learn how to use algorithms developed by other people, many of which are published in books and journals, as subroutines in your own programs. Eventually, you may find that other peole will want to use the algorithms that you have developed and you will have joined that special 'club' of modellers to which you can only belong if you are contributing to the development of algorithms and applications of models. You can do none of this unless you learn how to program the computer yourself, and, at best, package programs and special-purpose languages are half-way stages to the fuller understanding that you will need ultimately. The danger is that you will be content with the half-way stage simply because you do not know what lies beyond.

5.3 Using the computer

The direct answer to the question which is at the heading of this chapter is 'Yes'. The advantages of using a computer for modelling are so great that it would be foolish to embark on the task without giving yourself these advantages. There may be some merit in doing things in the most difficult way possible, but it is hardly sensible if your main purpose is to gain an understanding of the natural systems you are trying to model. Access to computers is now readily available, and they are even cheap enough for the dedicated modeller to buy one for himself. To underline the point, however, let us review the advantages of using the computer.

The most obvious advantage lies in the speed with which calculations can be done. The modern computer can do more calculations in seconds than we used to be able to do manually in months, or even years. The calculations will also be correct; in the modern computer, the chance that the computer has made an arithmetical error is so small that it can be virtually neglected. That does not mean to say, however, that every calculation will be correct, because you may well have made a mistake in the program which you have asked the computer to obey. If there is a mistake, the speed of calculation generally means that very little is lost as you can simply ask the computer to repeat the calculation with a correct program. If you make a mistake in either the arithmetic or the design of your model when working manually, it may take you days, weeks, or months to re-do the calculations. Speed of computation is, therefore, a very definite advantage. There are some kinds of models which we simply could not use without computers because the calculations would take so long to do that the need for the model would have gone before we could complete them.

Speed is not, however, the most important advantage. All models require some data, and, in order to use your data, you will have to make them available to the computer. Input of data to computers is usually done by means of punched cards, punched paper tape, or, nowadays, directly through a keyboard or on-line device. The computer stores these data, usually on magnetic tape or disks. The magnetic tape may be a special and expensive kind of tape used only on computers, but it can also be the kind of tape which is used on hi-fi systems in cassettes. Similarly, the magnetic disks can be expensive fixed or removable disks which are specially adapted for use on computers, or they may be cheap 'floppy' disks which are now used on a wide variety of machines such as word-processors. Whatever the medium used, once the data have been made machine-readable, they are available for any subsequent use by the computer and can be transferred readily from one computer to another. The simple act of making the data machine-readable or of inputting them to the computer has added those data to an ever-increasing library of available data for the modeller to use. Other modellers may find that the data that you have contributed to this computer-held data-base are valuable to them. You, in turn, may find that some important data that are missing from those available to you have been contributed by another modeller and are held within the data-base. The computer has completely transformed our ability to store and use data and information. Our old methods of data storage, using notebooks and paper files, were actually ways of losing data because it was so difficult to extract the data from where we had put them for safe-keeping that, to all intents and purposes, they were unusable.

Even more important, then, than the speed of computation given by the use of the computer is the use of the machine as a data-base and as a means of communication with data held in other computer-orientated data-bases. As the capability of holding large amounts of data in readily accessible form increases, together with the improvement in information theory necessary for the efficient retrieval and updating of the data, we may expect the computer to become still more valuable as a source of information for our models. Associated improvements in the transmission of information from one device to another will enable us to communicate with remote sources of data, both to interrogate the data files and to extract those data which are relevant to our particular problems. PRESTEL, which marks some early experiments in this direction using the domestic TV receiver, is but the first sign of an information revolution which will transform the task of the modeller.

Just as the ability to store data in a computer is more important than the speed with which computations can be done, there is an even more important reason for using the computer. The only way in which a computer can be made to work is through a completely unambiguous set of instructions which we call a program. Every program is a detailed list of precise instructions arranged in a particular order, and intended to define exactly what is to be done and in what sequence. The computer program, therefore, provides an exact record of what has been done and how. By keeping copies of these programs, you can retain a record of your past work that has never been achievable in any other way. Even if you come back to a particular piece of work many years later, you will still be able to discover exactly what it was you did in the construction of the model, as well as the data that you used. What is more, if you want to communicate the details of your work to another modeller, the most effective way of making that communication is through an exchange of computer programs. By examining the program and the associated data, you will be able to observe details of the modelling process which are unlikely ever to be included in any written record. Even better, you can run the model on your own computer and compare the way it works and the results with your own modelling. Computer programs and algorithms, once regarded as a necessary evil, have turned out to be the principal advantage to be derived from the use of computers. These algorithms represent a vast storehouse of knowledge which is available to you only if you are willing to take the first step of learning to program computers for yourself. Having learnt, you will find to your surprise that you have been given a new and powerful medium for keeping records of your research and for communicating the results of that research to others who have taken the same step.

You cannot profit from any of these advantages without learning to make the best possible use of computers. Computers are, therefore, a very necessary part of modelling. If you cannot program and use a computer, start learning today. The process is not entirely painless, but programming languages have an enormous intellectual appeal once you have got past the first difficulties.

6 How do I know when to stop?

6.1 Re-examination of objectives

In one sense, of course, there is no need for you to stop modelling any problem. As your knowledge of the concepts which lie behind the problem increases, and as you incorporate these concepts within a framework of conceptual variation, so your perception of the linkages within the model, and from your model to other systems, will increase. There is no reason why this process of intellectual development should ever stop, supposing that you retain an interest in the original problem and are not diverted to some quite different activity. You should not expect your progress to be smooth and regular. There will sometimes be long periods when you seem to be getting nowhere, and when all attempts at improvement of the existing model result in failure. There will be other times when you make spectacular progress, and when ideas seem to come tumbling out of your mind faster than you can implement them. Inspiration will come from reading the papers or books of other people engaged in modelling, from discussions with colleagues, while walking the dog, or, most frustratingly, in the middle of the night. If you are not careful, you may well find that modelling is beginning to take over your life!

From time to time, however, and preferably fairly regularly, it pays to look back at your original objectives. Have you achieved what you set out to do? If so, while it may be tempting to pursue some aspect of the model which has been revealed while you were constructing it, there may be some more important tasks to occupy you. There may, for example, be some other problems which you might try to solve by modelling. Alternatively, there may be some other scientific tasks or skills which you should now develop. You, as a thinking human being, should remain in firm control of the tasks and activities that might otherwise dominate you. Models are only one small part of the whole intellectual excitement of science, and need to be kept firmly in perspective.

Re-examination of your original objectives may also reveal that you have allowed the heady pleasure of playing with the model to divert you from your original purpose. If so, then you have an opportunity to get your model, and your interests in the model, back into the right direction. The greatest danger is that you will have allowed your thinking about the original problem to become dominated by one particular model family. You may even have gone so far as to believe that your model is 'real' as opposed to being a caricature and simplification of reality. It may be time, therefore, to stop developing one model and to start developing a new model of the same problem, derived from a quite different model family. When you have worked with several different models of the same system, you will be able to compare the output from the models under broadly comparable conditions. The most important question then to be answered is 'Which of these models is most appropriate for meeting the objectives of my research'?

6.2 Sensitivity analysis

In addition to the re-examination of the relevance of your models to the objectives of your research, there is another activity which should be incorporated as an almost continuous feature of the modelling itself. The sensitivity of each model that you build should be tested by making small changes to the basic parameters and looking at the corresponding changes in the output variables. Some modellers leave this test of sensitivity until towards the end of the modelling process, but most experienced modellers begin their sensitivity analysis as soon as they have a working approximation, and there are some excellent examples of the advantages of this procedure, e.g. Miller *et al.* [52]. Marked differences in the sensitivity of the output variables to small changes in the basic parameters help to identify those variables for which increased precision in the estimates of the values of the parameters is desirable. Greater attention can then be given to those parts which are most likely to be improved by further research, or by modifications in the form of the model. A program of continuous experimentation as the relationships are being built helps the modeller to keep in close touch with the implications of his model, and with the conceptual variation with which he is concerned. If this experimentation is left until the end of the active modelling phase, many important clues to the improvement of the model may be missing, and the process will be much less efficient.

Sensitivity analysis should not be confined to the alteration of only one parameter at a time. Simultaneous alteration of several of the parameters and coefficients of the model will enable the modeller to detect the effect of interactions between the corresponding changes. Indeed, without tests of these interactions, the knowledge gained about the sensitivity of the model may be seriously deficient. Fortunately, there is a well-researched application of experimental design to the problem of determining the effects of factors and their interactions, particularly when the experiments can be carried out sequentially. Sensitivity analysis, with the aid of experimental designs, can, therefore, be done very efficiently, and as part of a carefully designed programme of research [53].

As the models which are being developed with the aid of a continuous sensitivity analysis become increasingly more reliable and more stable, the sensitivity analysis itself begins to take on a rather different role. Now, the main emphasis will be in testing the response of the model to extrapolation from the known data which have been used to build the model. How does the model behave when some of the driving variables are extrapolated? Are there some particular combinations of these extrapolated variables which cause the model to collapse? If so, is this because there is something inherently wrong with the structure of the model? Use of some of the best-known procedures for fitting curves to existing data, for example, can sometimes suggest relationships which become wildly unstable for only limited degrees of extrapolation, and it may be preferable to fit a relationship which gives a poorer fit to existing data but ensures a more reasonable response for limited amounts of extrapolation. Similarly, the analysis may reveal particular combinations of variables for which there are marked discontinuities in the performance of the model. Any such discontinuities will often limit the practical use of the model, and will cast doubts on its conceptual validity.

6.3 Verification

When you have a model which has been tested thoroughly for sensitivity, and for which you have made regular checks on the relevance of the model to the objectives of your research, the modelling enters a new phase, i.e. that of verification. If all has gone well, you should now have one or more models which simulate in different ways the natural system in which you are interested. It is time now to see if these models behave in ways which fit broadly with your expectations of how the real system actually does behave. Similarity in behaviour of the models and the natural system, at least for the known parts of that behaviour, is comforting, and gives some limited degree of confidence in the outcome of the modelling. The problem arises when one or more of the models behave in ways which do not fit with your expectations. You now have to decide whether the difference arises because there is something wrong with the model(s), or because of some fault in the reasoning or the programming. Alternatively, the real system which you are seeking to model may behave in a counter-intuitive way, so that the behaviour of your model is a correct expression of the logic incorporated into your synthesis, and it is your expectation or perception of the real system which is at fault. While there is obviously little to be gained from continuing to work with a model which is obviously wrong, it would be equally wrong to throw out a model merely because it does not confirm our prejudices.

Verification usually takes the form of further experiments of the kind which were done during the sensitivity analysis, but concentrating now on the model behaviour in response to attempts to 'manage' the system in ways which are relevant to our original objectives. Again, however, the main aim of the verification, as for sensitivity analysis, is to suggest ways in which the model can be improved and the original research objectives furthered.

6.4 Validation

Having reached this stage, it is tempting to regard the work as complete, but, if modelling is to be included as a part of scientific research, as opposed to an exercise in metaphysics or mythology, there is one final and essential phase. Our model, or models, must be tested formally by a direct appeal to nature. Unless we are willing to make the step of deriving a non-trivial prediction from our model, as a hypothesis about the way in which the real system behaves under some combination of circumstances, we cannot be said to be scientific. We must seek, then, some way of testing the validity of our model by using it to make a prediction about the real-world system which we can then check by direct experiment, or by reference to already-collected data. We begin, therefore, by an examination of the model to see if we can construct some explicit tests of hypotheses which may be made on the real system.

There is one very tempting trap to be avoided. In almost all cases, we will have had access to data about the real system in the construction of the model. These data will have been used to estimate the values of coefficients and parameters of the model. Indeed, the parameters may have been derived from an extensive analysis of the data, as in regression and variance component models. Any future test must be made against another set of data, either collected specially in order to test our hypotheses, or, as can sometimes be arranged, by using only part of the available data to estimate the model parameters. Scientists often feel that they should always use all of the available data when deriving their models, but it is frequently more efficient to use only some of the data and to retain the rest for testing the validity of the model later. Where data are particularly extensive, it may even be possible to divide the data into several distinct sets which can be used to build a variety of completely independent models and then test them. However the end result is achieved, it is essential that one or more completely independent sets of data are used to test the validity of any model.

A particular advantage of models is that they can often be used experimentally to derive tests of hypotheses which are critical, in the sense that they advance the whole research programme towards the originally defined objectives. Synthesis of models stands between the day-to-day management of the real system and the experiments which are done on that system. It is usually easier and cheaper to do experiments on the model system, so that a major research programme can often be simulated on a well-constructed model, leading to a small number of quite critical experiments which must be done on the real-world system. The results of these real-world experiments not only contribute to scientific publication, but also feed back into the re-design of the simulation, either by suggesting new experiments or by suggesting a re-formulation of the structure or family of the model. Again, the use of efficient experimental designs will greatly improve the ease with which we can do experiments on the models or on the real-world system. Such designs will also greatly improve the understanding that we derive from the experiments, by enabling us to explore the complex interactions between variables and the role of feedback mechanisms.

Appendix: Modelling checklist

This appendix is reproduced from a pamphlet in the Institute of Terrestrial Ecology Statistical Checklist series. Single copies of checklists can be obtained, at a cost of 30p, from the Publications Officer, Institute of Terrestrial Ecology, 68 Hills Road, Cambridge CB2 1LA (enclose a stamped addressed envelope with your order). Bulk supplies are available for institutes and organizations wishing to use these checklists for wider internal circulation. Copies are available in multiples of 20 at £3 per pack, post paid. Checklists so far issued include: (1) Design of experiments; (2) Sampling; (3) Modelling.

Stating the objectives
1. Have you stated clearly and explicitly the objectives of the research and the reasons for doing it?
2. Have you translated these objectives into precise questions that the research may be expected to answer?

Relevance of Modelling
3. Are you satisfied that modelling of some part of the system through a formal statement of relationships in physical or mathematical terms will help in the achievement of the objectives of the research?
4. Are sufficient accurate data available to allow models to be tested? If not, can such data be collected?
5. Are the relationships envisaged by this research complex in the sense that they involve feedback and non-linearity?
6. Is the model intended to provide a simulation of the natural system for further experimentation and as a synthesis to guide further research?
7. Is the model intended to help with the making of decisions about the natural system?
8. Is the model intended to integrate and test the compatibility of information about the system which has already been collected?
9. Do you have any doubts about the feasibility of modelling the system which relates to the research objectives?
10. If so, have you consulted someone with modelling expertise in your field of research in order to confirm the feasibility of the modelling approach to your particular problem?
11. Have you estimated the time and cost of producing models and established that the requisite resources are available?

Word model
12. Have you identified and defined the boundaries of the problem and of the system to be modelled?
13. Have you written a verbal description of the assumed relationships between the various entities of the problem, using the simplest language possible?

69

14. Has this verbal description been seen by a cross-section of appropriate experts and been agreed by them as an adequate description?
15. Does the verbal description identify the parameters which you consider to be essential to the solution of the problem and give some preliminary indication of the relative importance of these parameters?
16. Does the verbal description give any indication of possible qualitative solutions which might subsequently be compared with the quantitative solutions to be derived from modelling?
17. Have you translated the relationships described in the word model into diagrams, using one of the established conventions for such diagrams?
18. Have you identified distinct sub-systems in the problem which can be examined separately, but which need to be connected together?

Dynamic models
19. Have you considered the possibility of modelling the relationships described in the word model by one or more differential or difference equations?
20. Have you identified the necessary input, state and output variables for such equations?
21. Have you identified the appropriate time steps for the solution of the equations?
22. Does the word model make explicit the non-linearity of the relationships between the model parameters?
23. If not, are there some alternative ways of expressing this non-linearity which you would like to test?
24. Do the equations express the necessary degree of feedback to meet the requirements described by the word model?

Matrix models
25. Have you considered the formulation of the model in terms of a matrix or matrices?
26. If so, do any of the well-known matrix formulations meet the requirements described by the word model? Does the matrix notation simplify the mathematical presentation and solution of the problem?
27. Do eigenvalue and eigenvector solutions of the component matrices define properties of the model which are relevant to the solution of the original problem?

Markov models
28. Does a Markov model, as a special type of matrix model, have any application in the solution of the original problem?
29. If so, do you have any appropriate procedure for estimating the probabilities for the transitions from one state to another?
30. Does the model have closed states, i.e. is it an absorbing Markov chain?
31. If so, are you concerned to estimate the absorption times and probabilities?
32. If the model does not have absorbing states, i.e. is an ergodic Markov chain, are you concerned to estimate the limiting probabilities and the mean passage times from one state to another?

Stochastic models
33. Does the model formulation envisaged by the word model require the introduction of stochastic elements?

34. If so, can these stochastic elements be estimated for non-linear relationships?
35. Does the model require the estimation of several variances?
36. If so, do you know how to structure the collection of data so as to obtain unbiased estimates of those variances?
37. Can your model be structured so as to make use of the well-tested methods of least-squares estimation, e.g. analysis of variance or multiple regression analysis?
38. Are the estimates of the parameter values derived from your model independent of each other?

Multivariate models
39. Does your word model envisage the simultaneous evaluation of many variables or attributes?
40. If so, is the main purpose of your model to derive the most parsimonious representation of the variables in multivariate space, and a subsequent ordination of the model elements in the essential dimensions of that space?
41. Is the main purpose of your model to discriminate between *a priori* groupings of the model elements, and to allocate new elements to those groupings?
42. Is the main purpose of your model to find discontinuities in the multivariate space required to describe the variation of the model elements, and so to perform a cluster analysis of those elements?
43. Is the main purpose of your model to investigate the relationships between two or more groups of variables, for example by canonical correlation analysis?

Optimization models
44. Can the essential criteria of the word model be expressed in terms of game theory?
45. If so, can you evaluate the outcomes of the various strategies which are available to the opponents in the game model?
46. Does a saddle-point exist in the choice of strategies, i.e. a single strategy for each opponent which should always be played?
47. If not, what combination of strategies represents the optimum response to the conflict of issues between the opponents?
48. Can the search for an optimum strategy be developed within the constraints of a mathematical programming model?
49. If so, can the objective function and the constraints be expressed as linear equations or inequalities?
50. If either the objective function or the constraints have to be expressed as non-linear equations or inequalities, does an appropriate method of solution exist?
51. Does the search for an optimum solution have to take into account the need to retain the widest possible range of options for future solutions, i.e. indicate the need for a dynamic programming solution?

Catastrophe theory
52. Does the word model indicate any of the useful properties of catastrophe theory models, i.e. bimodality, discontinuity, hysteresis and divergence?
53. Can the delay in the jump from one state of the system to another, i.e. the

hysteresis, be expressed as a crossing of a singularity in the catastrophe surface?

54. Can the divergence between the outcomes of changes in the control variables be shown to arise from paths on either side of a catastrophe manifold?

Sensitivity analysis

55. Will you test the sensitivity of your model to small changes in the basic parameters of the model?

56. If so, will marked differences in the sensitivity of the output variables to these small changes help to identify those variables for which increased precision of estimation is desirable?

57. Will the sensitivity analysis be extended to the simultaneous alteration of parameters and coefficients so as to test the interaction of such changes?

58. Are you aware of the experimental designs which enable such tests to be made efficiently and without bias?

59. Will the sensitivity analysis be incorporated as a regular feature of the modelling procedure from the very beginning?

60. Will the sensitivity analysis identify any discontinuities in the performance of the model which would limit the practical use of the model?

Verification

61. Will you develop several models simultaneously, preferably from different model families, so that you can compare the output from the models under broadly comparable conditions?

62. Will these models behave in a way which fits broadly with your expectations?

63. If not, is this likely to be because of some fault with the model(s)?

64. Is it possible that the real system which you are seeking to model behaves in a counter-intuitive way?

65. Will verification of the model suggest any improvements which could be made to the research and to the modelling procedure?

Validation

66. Have you established which data are to be used in your model and ensured that independent data will be used to test the validity of your model?

67. Will the model which you construct suggest any explicit tests of hypotheses which might be made on the real system?

68. If so, are any of these tests critical in the sense that they significantly advance the research towards the originally-defined objectives.

69. Are you aware of the experimental designs which may improve the efficiency of these tests of the real system?

Computing

70. Have you investigated the computer facilities which are available to help with the modelling of your problem?

71. Do these facilities include any special-purpose modelling languages?

72. If so, have you investigated the applicability of these languages to your particular problem?

73. Are you intending to use a general-purpose computer language (e.g. BASIC, FORTRAN, APL. ALGOL) for the modelling of your problem?

74. If so, have you enquired about the existence of subroutines and algorithms which might simplify the task of programming your application?
75. Does the computer you intend to use provide for interactive facilities. e.g. through a computer terminal?
76. If not, is the time between submitting a request for a run and receiving the results short enough to allow you to make progress with the modelling task, i.e. less than 1–2 hours?

Exploration of model
77. When one or more models are complete, have you planned the uses of the models and the exploration of the consequences of changes in the input variables?
78. If so, are you aware of the experiment designs which may considerably simplify the exploration?
79. Have you thought through the possible uses of the simulation you hope to achieve?

Documentation
80. Have you provided for adequate documentation of the various stages of the modelling so that other research workers can benefit from your experience?
81. Have you planned the form of publication of the results of the modelling so that these results will be useful to decision-makers and administrators (if appropriate) as well as to scientists?

The final (and most important) question
82. If you are in any doubt about the purpose of any of the questions in this checklist, should you not obtain some advice from a modeller with experience of your field of research before continuing?

There is usually little that an expert advisor can do to help you once you have committed yourself to a particular approach.

Bibliography
If any of the questions in this checklist refer to theoretical concepts with which you are unfamiliar, further information can be found in the following texts:

Arnold, G.W. and de Wit, C.T. (1976), *Critical evaluation of systems analysis in ecosystems research and management*, Pudoc, Wageningen.

Converse, A.O. (1970), *Optimization*, Holt, Rinehart and Winston, New York.

Dent, J.B. and Blackie M.J. (1979), *System simulation in agriculture*, Applied Science Publishers, London.

De Wit, C.T. and Goudriaan, J. (1974), *Simulation of ecological processes*, Pudoc Wageningen.

Halfon, E. (1979) *Theoretical systems ecology*, Academic Press, New York.

Hall, C.A.S. and Day, J.W. (1977), *Ecosystem modelling in theory and practice*, Wiley, New York.

Jeffers, J.N.R. (1972), *Mathematical models in ecology*, Blackwell, Oxford.

Jeffers, J.N.R. (1978), *An introduction to system analysis: with ecological applications*, Arnold, London.

Maynard Smith, J. (1974), *Models in ecology*, Cambridge University Press.

Poston, T. and Stewart, I. (1978), *Catastrophe theory and its applications*, Pitman, London.

References

[1] McKeague, C.P. (1978), *Elementary algebra*, Academic Press, New York, London.

[2] Volterra, V. (1926), Variazone & fluttuazini del numero d'individui in specie animali conviventi. *Atti Accad. naz. Lincei Memorie* (*ser 6*), **2**, 31–113.

[3] Maynard Smith, J. (1974), *Models in ecology*, Cambridge University Press, London, Cambridge.

[4] Snedecor, G. and Cochran, W.G. (1980), *Statistical methods*, 7th edn, Iowa State University, Iowa.

[5] Lohnes, P.R. and Cooley, W.W. (1968), *Introduction to statistical procedures: with computer exercises*, John Wiley and Sons, New York, London.

[6] Davies, R.G. (1971), *Computer programming in quantitative biology*, Academic Press, London, New York.

[7] Daniel, C. and Wood, F.S. (1971), *Fitting equations to data*, John Wiley and Sons, New York, London.

[8] Leith, H. (1972), *Interactive data analysis*, John Wiley and Sons, New York, London.

[9] McNeil, D.R. (1977), *Interactive data analysis*, John Wiley and Sons, New York, London.

[10] May, R.M. (1976), Simple mathematical models with very complex dynamics. *Nature, London*, **261**, 459–67.

[11] De Wit, C.T. and Goudriaan, J. (1974), *Simulation of ecological processes*, Centre for Agricultural Publishing and Documentation, Wageningen.

[12] Jeffers, J.N.R., Howard, Doreen M. and Howard, P.J.A. (1976), An analysis of litter respiration at different temperatures. *J. R. Statist. Soc.*, (*C*), **25**, 139–46.

[13] Forrester, J.W. (1961), *Industrial dynamics*, Massachusetts Institute of Technology Press, Massachusetts.

[14] Odum, H.T. (1972), An energy circuit language for ecological and social systems: its physical basis. In *Systems analysis and simulations in ecology*, Vol II (Patten, B.C., ed.), Academic Press, New York, London.

[15] Grossman, S.I. (1977), *Calculus*, Academic Press, New York, London.

[16] Flanders, H., Korfhage, R.R. and Price, J.J. (1974), *A second course in calculus*, Academic Press, New York, London.

[17] Searle, S.R. (1966), *Matrix algebra for the biological sciences*, John Wiley and Sons, New York, London.

[18] Anton, H. (1977), *Elementary linear algebra*, 2nd edn, John Wiley and Sons, New York, London.

[19] Rorres, C. and Anton, H. (1977), *Applications of linear algebra*, John Wiley and Sons, New York, London.

[20] Strong, G. (1976), *Linear algebra and its applications*, Academic Press, New York, London.

[21] Anton, H. and Kolman, B. (1978), *Applied finite mathematics*, 2nd edn, Academic Press, New York, London.

[22] Poston, T. and Stewart, I. (1978), *Catastrophe theory and its applications*, Pitman Publishing Ltd, London.

[23] Seifert, H. and Threlfall, W. (1980), *A textbook of topology*, Academic Press, New York, London.

[24] Holling, C.S. (ed.) (1978), *Adaptive environmental assessment and management*, John Wiley and Sons, Chichester.

[25] Holling, C.S. (1981), *Sciences for public policy and highlights of adaptive environmental assessment and management*, R-23, Institute of Resource Ecology, University of British Columbia.

[26] Holling, C.S. and Chambers, R.D. (1973), Resources sciences: the nature of an infant. *Biosciences*, **23**, 13–20.

[27] Lewis, E.G. (1942), On the generation and growth of a population. *Sankhya*, **6**, 93–6.

[28] Leslie, P.H. (1945), On the use of matrices in certain population mathematics. *Biometrika*, **33**, 183–212.

[29] Lefkovitch, L.P. (1967), A theoretical evaluation of population growth after removing individuals from some age groups. *Bull. ent. Res.*, **57**, 437–45.

[30] Williamson, M.H. (1959), Some extensions in the use of matrices in population theory. *Bull. math. Biophys.*, **21**, 13–17.

[31] Usher, M.B. (1966), A matrix approach to the management of renewable resources, with special reference to selection forests. *J. appl. Ecol.*, **3**, 355–67.

[32] Usher, M.B. (1967/8), A structure for selection forests. *Sylva, Edinb.*, **4,7** 6–8.

[33] Usher, M.B. (1969), A matrix model for forest management. *Biometrics*, **25**, 309–15.

[34] Usher, M.B. (1969), A matrix approach to the management of renewable resources, with special reference to selection forests – two extensions. *J. appl. Ecol.*, **6**, 347–48.

[35] Lefkovitch, L.P. (1965), The study of population growth in organisms grouped by stages. *Biometrics*, **21**, 1–18.

[36] Lefkovitch, L.P. (1966), The effects of adult emigration on populations of *Lasioderme serricorne* (*F.*). (Coleoptera: Anobiidae). *Oikos*, **15**, 200–10.

[37] Pielou, E.C. (1969), *An introduction to mathematical ecology*, Wiley-Interscience, New York, London.

[38] Greig-Smith, P. (1964), *Quantitative plant ecology*, 2nd edn, Butterworths, London.

[39] Sprent, P. (1969), *Models in regression and related topics*, Methuen, London.

[40] Cormack, R.M. (1971), A review of classification. *J.R. Statist. Soc. (A)*, **134**, 321–67.

[41] Fisher, R.A. (1936), The use of multiple measurements in taxonomic problems. *Ann. Eugen.*, **7**, 179–88.

[42] Blackith, R.E. and Blackith, R.M. (1969), Variation of shape and of discrete anatomical characters in the morabine grasshoppers. *Aust. J. Zool.*, **17**, 697–718.

75

[43] Waloff, N. (1966), Scotch broom (*Sarothamnus scoparius* (L.) Wimmer) and its insect fauna introduced into the Pacific northwest of America. *J. appl. Ecol.*, **3**, 293–311.

[44] Van Dyne, G.M., Frayer, W.E. and Bledsoe, L.J. (1970), Some optimization techniques and problems in the natural resource sciences. In *Studies in optimization*, **1**, 95–124. Symposium on Optimization, Society for Industrial and Applied Mathematics, Philadelphia, Pennsylvania.

[45] Converse, A.O. (1970), *Optimization*, Holt, Rinehart and Winston, New York.

[46] Williams, J.D. (1966), *The compleat strategyst*, McGraw-Hill, London, New York.

[47] Jones, D.D. (1975), *The application of catastrophe theory to ecological systems*, IIASA Research Report RR-75-15.

[48] Sammet, J.E. (1969), *Programming languages: history and fundamentals*, Prentice-Hall, New Jersey.

[49] Kemeny, J.G. and Kurtz, T.E. (1968), *BASIC programming*, John Wiley and Sons, London, New York.

[50] Sanderson, P.C. (1973), *Interactive computing in BASIC*, Butterworths, London.

[51] Alcock, D. (1979), *Illustrating BASIC*, Cambridge University Press, Cambridge.

[52] Miller, D.R., Butler, Gail and Bramall, Lise (1976), Validation of ecological system models *J. environ. Manage.*, **4**, 383–401.
practical algorithms. PhD thesis, Sheffield City Polytechnic.

[54] Chaston, I. (1971), *Mathematics for ecologists*, Butterworths, London.

[55] Pearce, S.C. (1969), Multivariate techniques of use in biological research. *Expl Agric.*, **5**, 67–77.

[56] Hill, M.O. (1973), Reciprocal averaging, an eigenvector method of ordination. *J. Ecol.*, **61**, 237–49.

Index